ENJOYING
GOD FOREVER

Foundations
OF THE Faith

The
Westminster
Confession

ENJOYING

GOD FOREVER

Paul Smith

MOODY PRESS
CHICAGO

ISBN: 0-8024-7109-9

1 3 5 7 9 10 8 6 4 2

Printed in the United States of America

To my wife, Carreen, our son, Lucian,
and our three daughters,
Taleigh, Lindsay, and Miriam,
who have not merely survived
being part of a pastor's family,
but have taken genuine delight
in learning to enjoy God with me

CONTENTS

PREFACE

I have never quite determined whether I am at heart an Evangelical Christian raised in the Reformed tradition or a Reformed Christian raised in the Evangelical tradition. Indeed, I was well along in my theological and historical studies before I realized that the two could be distinguished. But while each has distinguishing features, I do not consider them to be in the least incompatible. The reason for this lies at the very heart of the historic term "Reformed." When Martin Luther's protest against certain aspects of Catholic belief and practice began to take root in Switzerland, a man by the name of Huldrich Zwingli and his colleagues (John Calvin's immediate predecessors) determined that the problems were systemic and that the church would have to be "re-formed" from its roots. To do this would require them to explore the Word of God in depth, and, casting aside all traditions and extrabiblical practices, make certain that everything they believed and practiced came directly from the Scriptures. This fundamentally biblical approach to faith and practice unites the Evangelical and Reformed traditions.

This is not to say that everyone in both traditions agrees on every point of doctrine. Differences in the interpretation and application of Scripture have led those who are in every way brothers and sisters in Jesus Christ down separate paths. Perhaps most obvious are the differences in understanding of the sacraments/ordinances and the interpretation of prophetic writings concerning the last days. But those are intramural debates. What we have in common is our understanding of the character of God, the person of Christ, the role of the Holy Spirit, the nature and purpose of creation, the doctrines of salvation and of the church, and most especially our commitment to Jesus Christ as Savior and Lord. All this grows out of our mutual acknowledgment of the fundamental authority of the Word of God.

Although the Westminster Confession is perhaps the most thorough and distinctive expression of Reformed doctrine, this book is intended to explore our common heritage, the beliefs and commitments that have made us one in Jesus Christ. As a result, I have not dealt with issues such as our approach to worship, the relationships of church and state, differences in church government, or other more controversial subjects addressed in the Westminster Confession, but not essential to our place in the body of Christ. The reader who would like to know more about the issues that defined that moment in the church's history may read the full text of the Confession in the appendix at the end of this book.

But my desire is to celebrate the heart of our faith and to invite every reader from any theological perspective to join in the adventure of coming to know God, to glorify Him, and to enjoy Him forever!

ACKNOWLEDGMENTS

I would especially like to thank my secretary, Mrs. Lynda Hurst, for faithfully transcribing my messages, serving as my liaison with the congregation and community, and for her work in preparing this manuscript for publication. And I would like to express my overwhelming gratitude to the remarkable members of West Side Presbyterian Church in Seattle, who forgive my failings, pray for me consistently, and dedicate themselves unequivocally to coming to know God and glorify Him with the anticipation of enjoying Him forever.

To Glorify God

and Enjoy Him

Forever

We live in a broken world. Anyone who does not recognize this will not be able to make sense of his own experience, let alone the confusing distortions of the world around him. But if it is clear that things are not what they should be, how can we make them better? To answer this question will require first of all that we understand who God is and what are His intentions. Then we must know what has gone wrong. And, finally, we need to know what God is doing, and what we may do, to restore the world lost in Eden.

The Westminster Confession of Faith was written for the precise purpose of answering these questions and leading us along the path to a world in which all things are ultimately made new. As we shall discover, God has had a plan all along. But we need to discover it and find our place within it.

After the Bible, few documents in human history have had a more profound effect upon the shaping of

Christian belief than The Westminster Confession of Faith, published in 1649. But to understand the impact of this magnificent work, we need to recognize it as a living document shaped by its own place in history, even as it in turn shaped subsequent history.

When the Westminster Assembly convened at Westminster Abbey in London on July 1, 1643, to consider the most effective form of government, worship, and belief for the Church of England, that great nation was being torn apart by a bitter civil war. Indeed, the very issues being addressed by the assembly had triggered the war.

A century earlier, the Protestant Reformation had come to England with the Act of Supremacy in which Henry VIII declared the church's independence from Rome. But this had been a political move with few serious spiritual consequences. When Mary Tudor, known to later history as "Bloody Mary," had tried to restore Catholicism in England through violent means, hundreds of Protestant leaders had fled, many to Geneva, Switzerland, where they came under the influence of John Calvin and John Knox, men who had been remarkably successful in integrating faith and life. Returning during the reign of Queen Elizabeth, they began to agitate for real change in the Church of England.

Convinced that a Reformation, to be worthy of the name, must involve a genuine change of heart, they began to call for purer standards of morality within the church, a purer doctrine and forms of worship, as well as a purging and purifying of the church's form of government. Such prodding soon earned them the nickname

"Puritans," a title that often carries a negative connotation today. But in fact, the Puritans were a sincere people who believed absolutely in the life-transforming power of God, and who believed that the gospel, if it is true, must radically affect every area of a person's life. They were committed to discipline their own lives to live in conformity with the laws of God, and they saw no reason that they should not seek to direct the whole of society toward the same goal. Their disdain for state control, however, began to unsettle the throne.

When Charles I became king, he was determined to force the Puritans, along with the Scottish Presbyterians, into conformity with the government and the Anglican Church. The independent-minded Scots rebelled, however. When Charles called for the election of a parliament to help press the war against them, to his great dismay the people elected a Puritan parliament that refused Charles's order to dissolve and raised its own army to defend against the king.

As the resulting civil war spread, this Puritan parliament decided the time had come to put its beliefs into action. In 1643, the House of Commons adopted an ordinance calling for the "settling of the government and liturgy of the Church of England (in a manner) most agreeable to God's Holy Word." After agreement from the House of Lords, an Assembly was convened at Westminster Abbey consisting of 121 of the most able and articulate Puritan ministers who could be found in England. Joined by thirty members of the parliament, and later by a half dozen Scottish Presbyterians with voice but no vote, the group set to work to reform the Church of England from the foundation up.

Not only did this group represent the intellectual cream of the British Isles, it was also deeply spiritual. One entire day of each month was spent in fasting and prayer and worship, while the body bathed its daily deliberations in diligent prayer as well. All points of view in debate had to be defended strictly on the basis of an able exposition of the Scriptures. In the accounts of the assembly chronicled by Robert Baillie, one of the Scottish commissioners, the reader finds almost palpable the sense that something extraordinary for the kingdom of God was taking place here.

Five and one-half years later, the assembly completed its work with a Directory for Worship, a Form of Church Government, a Psalter, and a magnificent Confession of Faith accompanied by Larger and Shorter Catechisms—series of questions and answers that summarized the primary doctrines of the Confession. The tides of war, however, ultimately removed the Puritans from power, and the Church of England abandoned the work of the assembly. But the Scottish ministers in attendance took it back to the Church of Scotland, where it was enthusiastically adopted. From there it eventually came to America in the migration that preceded our own Revolution. Although other statements of faith have taken their place alongside this one, few documents in the history of the Protestant Reformation can claim the degree of influence won by this brilliant exposition of the Word of God. It was, after all, developed from an unsurpassable formula: the finest minds, subject to the most yielded spirits, immersed in the revelation of God's holy Word.

The Shorter Catechism begins with the most fundamental question we will ever face, along with the most brilliant answer ever proposed. It asks, "What is the chief end of man?" Today we ask the same question in other words: Why do we exist? What are we here for? The Catechism supplies a most astonishing and encouraging answer: "Man's chief end is *to glorify God, and to enjoy him forever.*" Perhaps no more powerful and succinct statement of Christian purpose exists than that well-known declaration. The whole of the Confession explains what this means, why it is so important, how we may achieve it, and finally where we may find the joy and fulfillment for which our souls long.

In the end, the Westminster Confession of Faith is the story of the great adventure of the human race from Paradise Lost to Paradise Restored. I invite you to join me on this adventure. Our study of it will help us to understand where we are in this epic adventure leading to what God's Word promises will be "new heavens and a new earth, in which righteousness dwells" (2 Peter 3:13 NASB).

Chapter One

THE GOD

WHO SPEAKS

Of the Holy Scriptures

Westminster Confession, chap. I;
Psalm 19

*T*he steel gray November sky hid the sun from Ana as she headed across campus toward her favorite coffee shop. Around her was all the evidence that the season was changing. The wind snatched at the handful of leaves still clinging desperately to the sturdy branches, resisting to the last the inevitable change occurring within them. And she was changing too, whether she wanted to or not. She had anticipated the change, and she had welcomed it as she arrived on campus that fall, fresh from her home in the Midwest. But change was a mixed blessing, and she wasn't sure how she felt about all of it.

Her World Religion class had introduced her to what seemed like the most fundamental challenge to everything she had believed up to now. It wasn't that her studies demanded she throw out her Christian faith. It was just that she had now been exposed to so many other beliefs that she had begun to wonder seriously how she could believe that her faith was right and all the others were wrong.

How could a person really know what was true? She had her Bible, of course, but most of the other religions had sacred books as well. Why should she believe hers and disregard theirs? Wasn't it a bit naive to believe that the Bible was actually the inspired Word of God? It was a good book, of course, but wasn't it just a collection of man's best thoughts, pretty much like all the others? Besides, all such books seemed to reflect a rather mystical, pre-scientific age before we had the means to examine the world more carefully for ourselves. Why should she believe any of it?

Ana didn't know if she felt good or bad about this growing doubt. On the one hand it freed her from a sense that she ought to be some sort of slave to a mysterious God who claimed to be the Truth. Her studies seemed to give her more credit, to allow her to discern for herself what was right and wrong. On the other hand, wasn't that the temptation of Eve in the Garden of Eden? With a growing uneasiness she realized that if she couldn't count on the Bible, or some other source of authority and truth, it would be impossible to ever really know how things were, particularly in the moral and spiritual realms.

Ana's questions are not ones we should run from. It would be easiest for Christians to simply proclaim that the Bible is true and that's all there is to it. But how do we know that for certain? What if it isn't? Is there any chance we could be on the wrong track? Does anything separate the Bible from other religious books? Any nagging doubts we nurse regarding the Bible's truth claims will make us hesitant about a total commitment to follow the way it directs. How can we know the truth?

On my living room wall hangs an oil painting my wife and I purchased on Montmartre in Paris during our student days. It is a simple picture of two wooden boats beached just above the waterline beneath high and colorful clouds. I know nothing about the artist except his name, but periodically I wonder who he is or was, what if anything he wished to say in this painting, what sort of person he might have been, and whether his life and work have been significant.

That an artist exists (or existed) who is responsible for this painting is of course beyond question. To think otherwise would be absurd. Because of the picture's careful and complex construction and design, I do not think for a moment that it came into being by chance in a blinding thunderstorm or through the random movement of complex molecules in a primeval swamp. Furthermore, from the painting I can learn certain things about the artist. I see clearly demonstrated his artistic ability, his love for beauty, and perhaps his interest in boats.

But what he had in mind in creating this painting must remain a mystery to me unless I have a conversation with him—or speak to someone who has spoken with him, or perhaps find some documentation in which he recorded his intentions. In other words, for me to know his purpose, he would have to tell me. That is an obvious conclusion, but it has profound implications. I simply cannot know his mind unless he chooses to communicate with me. Short of this, any attempt to answer these questions about him or about his purpose or intentions would be sheer speculation on my part.

THE ARTIST WHO CREATED THE UNIVERSE

A mystery infinitely more important than this one involves the Artist responsible for the creation of which you and I are a part. That our Creator exists is absolutely beyond question. We are surrounded by His work; indeed, we participate in His creation in all its otherwise unexplained beauty and complexity. It is unthinkable that all this came about by chance.

Psalm 19 says, "The heavens declare the glory of God; the skies proclaim the work of his hands. Day after day they pour forth speech; night after night they display knowledge. There is no speech or language where their voice is not heard."

Every morning when you watch the sun come up, every evening when you see it descend through colorful clouds at the close of the day, every night when you see the constellations and reflect on the galaxies, you see God's wisdom and His sovereignty and His creative power displayed. There is no language in which that word is not heard, Psalm 19 says.

This has come to be known as "general revelation." It is what any observer can learn about the artist through examination of his work. The apostle Paul points out in his letter to the Romans that "what may be known about God is plain to them, because God has made it plain to them. For since the creation of the world God's invisible qualities—his eternal power and divine nature—have been clearly seen, being understood from what has been made, so that men are without excuse" (1:19–20). In other words, we have no excuse for failing to recognize the existence of God and His sovereignty and creativity. That is the most evident thing in the world.

But once we recognize that this particular artist is the sovereign Creator of the entire universe, we realize that our subsequent questions about His purpose and intent have become questions of enormous importance. They are not curiosities, as they may have been with my artist. What, for example, is this God really like? Why has He done what He has done? Is God fundamentally good or evil? If He is the author of life, on what does life depend? What is its purpose and its destiny? And what will we make of death? We find ourselves to be an integral part of this creation. What then is our purpose here? How do we fit in with the rest of creation? What might God expect of us? Will we be held accountable for our conduct? If so, how will we determine what particular actions are good or evil in His eyes? And what will be His response should we fail? One cannot help but recognize these questions as terribly significant.

Once they have been raised we begin to ask, Where could we possibly find answers to such questions? Here all our usual sources of knowledge fail us. We are often overwhelmingly dependent upon scientific observation. Nearly all the truth we will accept comes from this. But how can any science answer even one of those questions? It cannot. Science can only analyze and describe the material world, but all these questions lie completely off the map of the material world. Science has no tools to examine a spiritual world, should one exist. Science has no basis for making moral judgments. All it can say is what is, not whether it is right. Science has no way of declaring purpose. It has no way of looking beyond the material world at a phenomenon like death. If we want answers to those questions, science simply cannot provide them.

When science fails us, we often turn to philosophical speculation. We may think long and hard about the questions and try to make up some answers that seem reasonable. Some have done this brilliantly. But considering the importance of the questions, this seems a rather precarious approach. What if we are wrong? Are we really willing to stake our life and destiny on a guess?

COMMUNICATION FROM THE CREATOR

If we have been created as rational beings, we must have been made by a rational Creator, and it stands to reason He would want to communicate with us. When Job and his friends began speculating about the nature of good and evil and about what might be God's intent and purpose in life, God finally interrupted and said:

> Who is this that darkens my counsel with words without knowledge? . . . Where were you when I laid the earth's foundation? Tell me, if you understand. . . . On what were its footings set, or who laid its cornerstone—while the morning stars sang together . . . ? Have the gates of death been shown to you? . . . Tell me, if you know all this. (Job 38:2, 4, 6, 17a, 18b)

Let's be realistic, God is saying. How can you speak about things you have no opportunity to observe? The fact is, you're guessing. What do you really know about the origin of life? What do you know about the intentions of God? What do you know about the mystery of death? You have a lot of confidence for one who wasn't there! You may speculate, but deciding on something doesn't make it true, and it may prove a dangerous game if your life and destiny depend upon it.

With these words God silenced Job and his friends. But where does this leave us? If these questions lie beyond the scope of our knowledge, if neither the scientist nor the philosopher can tell us, are we condemned to ignorance concerning the most important questions the human race could possibly face? Many contemporary thinkers have concluded this. They are resigned to the necessity of people making up their own reality—taking a good guess and making the best of it.

But of course there is another option. It is possible that the Artist may tell us. He has made us in His image, after all, which means that we too are communicators, and it is not at all unlikely that He would speak to us. And the fact is, He is the only One who can know these things that lie beyond the range of human experience. Every question we have raised, God alone can answer. If He chooses to tell us, then we may know as well and order our lives accordingly. If not, understand this, *there is simply no way for us ever to know the truth for certain!* We need God to reveal Himself to us, or we must remain ignorant concerning everything of real importance in life. We need Him to tell us about His character, or we simply cannot know. We need Him to tell us what He expects of us, or we will certainly fail.

The central claim of Scripture is that the Bible is just such a revelation from God and it contains the answers to all those questions. From the moment God's finger traced on stone those Ten Essentials for His covenant people, through the conscious *"thus saith the Lord"* proclamations of His prophets, to the specific claim late in the New Testament that "all Scripture is inspired by God and is profitable for teaching, for reproof, for correction, for training in righteousness" (2 Timothy 3:16 NASB), the Bible lays claim to an inspiration that reveals the mind of God on all the most significant issues of life. Here, we are assured, we may learn the Truth that is otherwise totally inaccessible to us.

GOD'S WRITTEN WORD

On this solid bedrock the members of the Westminster Assembly laid the foundation for the Confession that has become the central expression of the Reformed faith. Mystics claimed that God had spoken to them directly. The Roman church had allowed the traditions of men an authority commensurate with the Holy Scriptures. But the Reformers were committed to found their faith solely on the authority of the Word of God revealed and recorded in the Bible.

The first chapter of the Confession begins with an observation about the limitations of general revelation:

> Although the light of nature, and the works of creation and providence do so far manifest the goodness, wisdom, and power of God, as to leave men unexcusable; yet are they not sufficient to give that knowledge of God, and of his will, which is necessary unto salvation.

In other words, we cannot know what God requires, nor can we have a relationship with Him, unless we know things He alone can tell us.

> Therefore it pleased the Lord, at sundry times, and in divers manners, to reveal himself, and to declare . . . his will

unto his church; and afterwards, for the better preserving and propagating of the truth, . . . to commit the same wholly unto writing. (I.I)

Quoting from the introduction to the book of Hebrews, the Westminster Assembly acknowledges that God has provided us with a specific and verbal revelation of His will. This will give them confidence to speak about God's intent and purpose for His creation.

So committed were these men to make the Scriptures their sole authority that they laid down one primary rule to guide themselves in all discussions: "What any man undertakes to prove as necessary, he shall make good out of Scripture." And every member of that assembly was required to take the following vow, which was read back to them every Monday morning for five and a half years while they worked on those documents: "I do seriously promise and vow, in the presence of Almighty God, that in this Assembly whereof I am a member, I will maintain nothing in point of doctrine but what I believe to be most agreeable to the Word of God ..."

This, then, was the foundation. The Westminster Confession of Faith would be built strictly on what the Bible actually says, not upon anyone's personal preferences, speculations, or private visions. Of course all of us bring to the Scriptures certain expectations and even prejudices that in turn color our interpretation of what we find there. These men shared that very human limitation. But it would be offset to some extent by the fact that they were a fairly large and diverse group who represented the best scholarship across England and Scotland, and primarily by the fact that they immersed their five and a half years of concentrated study in fervent prayer. Their goal was not to defend a system they had already come to believe, but rather to construct a new system that must at every point bear the scrutiny of careful biblical scholarship.

But a second major question looms. It may well be true that we can only know the Truth if God reveals it to us. But how do we know that the Bible is in fact that word? Is it unique among the world's religious documents? How do we know the Bible is God's Word? The Confession concludes that "the authority of the holy Scripture, for which it ought to be believed, and obeyed" (I.IV) depends wholly upon its being authored by God. It only has the kind of authority we need if God actually inspired it, not simply if a lot of bright men or women wrote it. So how may we be convinced that the Bible has in fact been written by God and may therefore be accepted as totally authoritative? To find an answer, we must begin by taking a closer look at the Book itself.

A beautiful passage in the Confession reflects on the fact that:

> The heavenliness of the matter [it goes consciously beyond the scope of earthly knowledge], the efficacy of the doctrine [it works!], the majesty of the style, the consent of all the parts, the scope of the whole (which is, to give all glory to God), the full discovery it makes of the only way of man's salvation, the many other incomparable excellencies, and the entire perfection thereof, are arguments whereby it doth abundantly evidence itself to be the Word of God. (I.V)

It is saying, first of all, that this is an astonishing Book. If you get to know it, you will be impressed!

THE POWER OF GOD'S WRITTEN COMMUNICATION

If you were to ask me how one might be convinced of the Bible's unique authority, I know unequivocally what my answer would be. It is not the same as I would have given in the past. In the past I would have given you all sorts of logical arguments. But what I would tell you today is this: (1) Read it; and (2) do it. Then come back and tell me if you are convinced.

A certain credibility grows as we read the Scriptures and become familiar with them. We begin to recognize their comprehensiveness, their profundity, and their relevance. All other arguments aside, we become more and more impressed with the wisdom and power of this book. The picture of reality that emerges from it is both consistent and beautiful. The more we understand and the more we practice it, the more we realize it is the best and most effective way to live.

The elegance and majesty in its account of the truth is unsurpassed in any other literature. The thoroughness in its account of salvation addresses every conceivable question and balances every apparent contradiction. How, for example, does one reconcile God's holiness and our sin? How can we be forgiven without violating God's holiness? In the Bible's account of salvation all such questions are addressed and answered with elegance and beauty. Scripture has a thoroughness in the account, a depth and unity, a level of insight into life found absolutely nowhere else. I have enjoyed the study of the world's religions, but they have no document like this one. It simply stands apart from all other documents in its wisdom and its grace. But you must read and seek to follow it before you will know that.

The Confession also reminds us of the consent of all its parts. This is a rather fascinating and particularly persuasive argument for its inspiration. In contrast to other religious documents, which often prove to be rather self-serving documents by a single author, the Bible is not a single book. It is an entire library of sixty-six books, written by some forty different authors spanning sixty generations, over the course of nearly sixteen hundred years, on three continents, and in three different languages. It includes the works of kings and peasants, of statesmen and philosophers, of poets and politicians, of scholars and common laborers.

They are writing about the most controversial issues ever addressed: questions of moral accountability and the existence of God, of the nature of humanity and the purpose of life, of what happens after death—the very questions to which we have been seeking answers. These topics have consistently inspired wildly divergent opinions from the world's greatest thinkers. Yet the biblical writers, without benefit of consultation, spoke with a common voice, giving a unified and consistent picture of life and of the universe, agreeing on the most controversial moral issues, telling a consistent story from beginning to end. Such a remarkable unity would be inexplicable aside from the conclusion that God's Spirit inspired each one of those writers with His consistent truth![1]

One could speak as well of historical accuracy, the fulfillment of prophecy, the testimony of Jesus Christ to the authority of the Word, or the necessity under which God Himself operates to reveal the truth. If He is its source and if He holds us accountable for it, then He operates under a self-imposed necessity to reveal it to us. In the end, however, the Confession concludes, "our full persuasion and assurance of the infallible truth and divine authority thereof, is from the inward work of the Holy Spirit bearing witness by and with the Word in our hearts" (I.V). It is the Holy Spirit at work in our hearts who finally convinces us of the Scripture's truth. Do you wish to know the truth? Then read the Bible and put it into practice. If you are willing, the day will come when He will convince you.

There remains a need for understanding the Word that God has revealed. Here too the Confession establishes that it is the Holy Spirit's role to illuminate God's Word (I.VI). This is a specific and limited role. In an age when individuals seek power or recognition by claiming new revelations from God's Spirit, it is important to note that the Scriptures themselves, confirmed by Jesus, warn against adding or subtracting anything from this body of revelation. The Spirit's job, as the Confession points out, is not to inspire new and private visions, but to interpret to our understanding what God has already revealed.

This will be necessary because some things in the Scriptures are more difficult to understand than others. However, the Confession says, "those things which are necessary to be known, believed, and observed for salvation, are so clearly propounded . . . that not only the learned, but the unlearned, in a due use of the ordinary means, may attain unto a sufficient understanding of them" (I.VII). In other words, all of us may understand the heart of the Scriptures if we come to them with the right spirit and with an understanding of one or two fundamental principles of interpretation.

It is true that the Scriptures require careful interpretation. There are times when our conclusions will conflict with those of others who equally respect God's Word. It is *not* true that all interpretations are equally valid. In such times, the Confession points out, Scripture must interpret itself: "When there is a question about the true and full sense of any Scripture ... it must be searched and known by other places that speak more clearly" (I.IX). That is the fundamental principle of biblical interpretation. When we find a difficulty in interpreting any particular passage, we must step back and look at the whole of Scripture and ask, How does this fit into the overall picture? Truth cannot contradict itself. Therefore proper interpretation will be recognized in the consistency of the whole.

All this is terribly significant. Knowing how and where to find the truth is absolutely essential. But in the end, *to know the truth is one thing—to submit our lives to that truth is something else entirely!* Our lives must certainly end in failure if we do not know the truth. But to yield our wills moment by moment in practical ways to the truth that God has revealed—in the way we deal with one another regardless of our feelings, in the way we approach our marriages, our relationships, our parents or our children, our friends, and our colleagues at work—this is the significant thing. The transformation that brings God's blessing comes when we are willing to submit to His will, to say, "I will tell the truth regardless of the cost," "I will be kind even to those who hurt me," "I will be diligent and faithful in my worship and service," "I will stop trying to justify my disobedience." Whatever God is dealing with in our hearts, we need to submit our will to the truth revealed in His Word. This, of course, is infinitely more important than simply knowing the truth.

God speaks the truth to us because He knows that if we will conform our lives to that truth, we will know His joy and delight. At the same time He knows that if we refuse to conform our lives to the truth, it will destroy us. We have in our hands one of the most incredible treasures that God could ever give—a revelation of His ultimate truth. We have as well the gift of His Spirit to illuminate it. It remains for us to be diligent in coming to know that Word and learning to trust it, for in it the very heart of God is revealed, and the pathway to life and joy is disclosed.

NOTE

1. This argument was made by Josh McDowell in *Evidence That Demands a Verdict,* Vol. 1 (San Bernardino, Calif.: Campus Crusade for Christ, 1972), 18–20.

Chapter Two

HAS GOD

LOST CONTROL?

Of the Sovereignty of God

Westminster Confession, chaps. II–V;
Isaiah 46

Jackson turned away from the television screen. He felt a wave of nausea sweep over him. A fear too horrifying to contemplate—a fear he had fought back several times over the past several weeks—had apparently just become a reality. Jackson, a physician in family practice, had recently volunteered his services for three months at a refugee camp in central Africa.

Overwhelmed by the level of suffering endured by innocent families, he had spent close to eighteen hours a day responding to malnutrition, disease, and often grotesque injuries suffered by these victims of the unending political strife. He had delivered several babies to women in the camp, wondering, even as he delighted in the soft cries of new life, what sort of chance they would have. But in three months, the people had become far more than sad or expressionless faces in a photojournalist's report. He had come to know many by name, and he found some justification for his investment when some actually smiled at his approach.

He had left the camp just four weeks earlier, and now television news was reporting that his worst fears had been realized. The camp had been overrun by rebels, and several hundred people, mostly old people, women, and children, had been massacred. TV news photos showed blood-covered bodies sprawled in the African dirt—people whose bodies he had recently nursed back to health. And to make matters worse, early reports suggested that there had been some casualties among international aid workers as well—his own colleagues. Jackson left the room numb with pain and disbelief. It was beyond his comprehension. He was a devout Christian, but he didn't know how in the world God could let something like this happen. Was he fooling himself into thinking that God was actually in control?

There is, at the very heart of the Christian faith, a doctrine upon which all other doctrines depend, and by which all other doctrines are measured. If it is established, then everything else we are encouraged to believe makes sense. If it is denied, then nothing else we believe can be defended. It is the doctrine of *the sovereignty of God* —a fundamental axiom that insists God is in absolute control of the universe.

Our problem is that nearly everything we observe in our world seems to contradict this supposed truth. There are, first of all, endless "natural" calamities like famines and floods, earthquakes and storms, accidents and plagues, all of which cause untold suffering and death in our world. These seem to strike innocent and guilty alike without reference to conduct or character.

Second, human history is characterized by our inhumanity toward one another. Cruel wars waged against whole populations seem only an expansion of brutal crimes perpetrated against individuals. Children suffer some of the most horrible tortures, while their adversaries too often go free.

How then can we maintain in good conscience that God is still in control? Yet we do maintain this. In declaring that God is sovereign, we say that He is in absolute control of the universe, and that He is absolutely independent of any other will or power. God does whatever He wills; nothing happens without His leave, and no action or decision of any other person or being can interfere with the accomplishment of His purpose. This is indispensable to what we believe.

GOD'S DECLARATION OF HIS SOVEREIGNTY

The Westminster Confession begins its account of God by stating:

> There is but one only, living, and true God, who is infinite in being and perfection, . . . working all things according to the counsel of his own immutable [or unchangeable] and most righteous will. (II.I)

The Confession goes on to say:

> God hath all life, glory, goodness, blessedness, in and of himself; and is alone in and unto himself all-sufficient. . . . He is the alone fountain of all being, of whom, through whom, and to whom are all things; and hath most sovereign dominion over them, to do by them, for them, or upon them whatsoever himself pleaseth. (II.II)

That language is from the seventeenth century, but the truth it expresses we can easily understand. The question is: How is it, in the light of our chaotic world with its senseless violence and elusive justice, that we can claim such unequivocal sovereignty in the governance of our God? I believe there are at least three answers. First of all, this is what God claims about Himself, and we need to begin there, no matter what else we do or do not understand. Acknowledging at the outset that His ways are complex and difficult to understand, God says through Isaiah the prophet in chapter 55, "As the heavens are higher than the earth, so are my ways higher than your ways and my thoughts than your thoughts" (v. 9). Then, having encouraged some intellectual humility on our part, He goes on to assure us,

> As the rain and the snow come down from heaven, and do not return to it without watering the earth and making it bud and flourish, so that it yields seed for the sower and bread for the eater, *so is my word that goes out from my mouth: It will not return to me empty, but will accomplish what I desire and achieve the purpose for which I sent it.* (Isaiah 55:10–11, italics added)

When we are facing devastating floods or snowstorms, it is not necessarily apparent what good they are accomplishing. Nevertheless, in due time all nourishment and productivity is drawn from that precipitation. Likewise, much that happens in our world may be initially devastating, and it may not be immediately apparent what it is accomplishing. Yet God assures us that ultimately every event is achieving His perfect will. This is our starting point. It is what God says about Himself.

If we are inclined, in our small arrogance, to challenge this, we would do well to read again those last four chapters from the book of Job, where God shoots a stream of hard questions at Job:

> Who is this that darkens my counsel with words without knowledge? . . . Where were you when I laid the earth's foundation? Tell me, if you understand. . . . Who shut up the sea behind doors when it burst forth from the womb? . . . Have you ever given orders to the morning, or shown the dawn its place . . . ? Have the gates of death been shown to you? . . . Tell me, if you know all this. What is the way to the abode of light? . . . Can you bind the beautiful Pleiades? Can you loose the cords of Orion? Can you bring forth the constellations in their seasons . . . ? Do you know the laws of the heavens? Can you set up God's dominion over the earth? . . . Will the one who contends with the Almighty correct him? (Job 38:2, 4, 8, 12, 17–19, 31–33; 40:2)

What, after all, do we really know about the ways of God? Are we honestly in a position to challenge the One who brought all things into being by the power of His word? I would certainly be out of my league trying to tell Tiger Woods how to play golf, or Vladimir Horowitz how to play the piano, or Stephen Hawking how to do quantum physics. Yet somehow I feel that I can challenge God on how He runs the universe!

OTHER EVIDENCES OF GOD'S SOVEREIGNTY

Of course we have more to assure us of His sovereignty than His own claim, although that might be sufficient. He is gracious to us, and we are able to see His sovereignty in His actions as well. Romans 1:19–20 reminds us that we are without excuse, since God's divine power and creativity are evident in what He has made. He has, after all, brought all things into being out of nothing (IV.I). Science has no other explanation for how things are here. The Bible tells us God brought everything into being by the sheer and awesome power of His word. He brought magnificent order out of chaos in our universe. Our examination of His creation reveals not only the immense and beautiful choreography of the galaxies, but the complete solar system that lies within an infinitesimal atom, investing it with incalculable atomic power. God is the source of all this. He has brought precision out of chaos. He is the source of this incredible mystery called life that animates His creation. Everywhere we look in the world around us, we see overwhelming evidence of His sovereignty.

He is also clearly the Lord of all He has made. He stands in judgment over it, as He did in cleansing His creation in the flood or raining volcanic fire on Sodom and Gomorrah. He sees our acts done in secret, like Cain's slaying of his brother or David's sin with Bathsheba, and visits His judgment appropriately. He withholds the rain, or sends the flood, or parts the waters at precisely the right moment to accomplish His purpose.

In a magnificent act of sovereignty He outlined in advance a detailed history for the descendants of Abraham. All the threats and assaults of great men and nations, all the powerful and threatening forces of our world have not been able to stay His hand from the accomplishment of His promised preservation of His people. "Is anything too hard for the Lord?" He asked in promising a child to the barren, ninety-year-old Sarah (Genesis 18:14). And indeed the next year she bore a child. Although God does not always do what we anticipate or what we desire, again and again He proves His ability to accomplish His purpose against all odds. God is indeed sovereign.

Furthermore, even if He had never spoken to us and we were devoid of evidence of His sovereignty, we must recognize that sovereignty is necessary to His very being. Consider: He is the source of all. Everything exists by His will alone. Nothing can exist or act except He conceives and sustains it. How then could anything be beyond His power? He is like the author of a book who creates his own characters and places them in situations of his own choosing. There is no question that the author, who is in complete control, will be able to bring about the final conclusion he desires, regardless of the perils and complications that jeopardize the characters.

Such absolute power in an author is perhaps harmless enough. In our world it would be dreadful power in the hands of a lesser architect, but in the hands of a good God, this sovereignty is a good thing. It is a power that delivers us from all our fears, instills confidence in us in any circumstance, frees us to enjoy or appreciate everything He brings into our lives, and inspires us, if we trust Him, with a breathless anticipation for what is yet to come. What has the Author written as the final chapter of our lives?

"God the great Creator of all things," the Westminster Confession reminds us, "doth uphold, direct, dispose, and govern all creatures, actions, and things, from the greatest even to the least, by his most wise and holy providence, according to his infallible foreknowledge, and the free and immutable counsel of his own will, to the praise of the glory of his wisdom, power, justice, goodness, and mercy" (V.I).

If you and I really grasp the sovereignty of God, it has

to be tremendously reassuring to realize that, no matter what it looks like to us, everything in our world happens because God means for it to happen. Nothing can intervene, and nothing may escape His control. "Remember," He says once again through Isaiah, "I am God, and there is no other; I am God, and there is none like me. I make known the end from the beginning, from ancient times, what is still to come." In other words, "Things are not out of My control." He continues, "I say: My purpose will stand, and I will do all that I please. . . . What I have said, that will I bring about; what I have planned, that will I do" (Isaiah 46:9–11).

MAN'S FREE WILL

Of course this raises the question of our human freedom. Do we really have free choices if God is in absolute control? We shall address this problem in more depth in chapter 4, but it is worth noting that there is a problem whichever way we turn in regard to this issue. It would seem that either human beings have true freedom, in which case our choices limit His control, or else our human freedom is simply an illusion. But if the latter is the case, then we are forced to say that God Himself is responsible for the suffering and the evil in our world. How will we reconcile these two apparently contradictory doctrines of human freedom and God's sovereignty?

Interestingly, the Bible never attempts to reconcile them. Nor does it seem to recognize a contradiction between them. The Bible speaks as forthrightly about our freedom as it does about God's control. Perhaps the most we can say is that God's control is a good deal larger than our freedom. He seems able to encompass all our choices within the larger embrace of His sovereign will. For example, after Joseph's brothers sold him into slavery, he ended up in prison in Egypt. Much later, and quite improbably, he became prime minister. In explaining this remarkable turn of events, Joseph told his brothers, "You intended to harm me, but God intended it for good to accomplish what is now being done, the saving of many lives" (Genesis 50:20) You see, they had freely chosen to do an evil thing, but God used it to accomplish something good.

The whole story of Esther, in which the name of God is never mentioned, is a story of God's hidden providence. Haman, you will recall, plotted the death of Mordecai and the extermination of the Jews, but what happened? All his choices were reversed one by one by the circumstances. His choices led to the honoring of Mordecai and his own death and the death of those who joined in his intended pogrom against the Jews.

On the Day of Pentecost, Peter revealed how the particular and evil actions purposed by those who crucified Jesus served nonetheless to accomplish God's plan. "Jesus of Nazareth," he says, "was a man accredited by God to you by miracles, wonders and signs, which God did among you through him, as you yourselves know. *This man was handed over to you by God's set purpose and foreknowledge;* and you, with the help of wicked men, put him to death by nailing him to the cross" (Acts 2:22–23, italics added). You see, God never lost control, even though they had chosen an evil deed. Reflecting on all this a few days later, the believers acknowledged God's amazing sovereignty with the observation, "Indeed Herod and Pontius Pilate met together with the Gentiles and the people of Israel in this city to conspire against your holy servant Jesus, whom you anointed." They made particular choices in their own freedom concerning this Jesus, but in fact he concluded, "They did what your power and will had decided beforehand should happen" (Acts 4:27–28).

THE TENSION: GOD'S SOVEREIGNTY AND MAN'S FREE WILL

As the Westminster Confession explains it: "Although, in relation to the foreknowledge and decree of God, the first Cause, all things come to pass immutably, and infallibly"—they are going to happen because God has determined it—"yet, by the same providence, he ordereth them to fall out, according to the nature of second causes, either necessarily, freely, or contingently" (V.II). In other words, God regularly uses our freely chosen actions in the accomplishment of His immutable will. And that is a mystery we cannot comprehend. We can only see it at work. You understand, there is no way that what He has determined will fail to happen. He assures us of that time and again. But the fascinating thing about God's sovereignty is that all of our choices, for good or for evil, help to bring about God's good end. This is true not only of our sins, as in the illustrations we have just seen in the Scriptures, but also of our acts of obedience and our prayers.

Christians often ask why they should pray if God has already determined the outcome. The answer is that He has told us to pray, and that our prayers may be the instrument God uses to bring about the result. No one would deny that Abraham's acts of obedience led to the establishment of God's covenant with His people. The whole Bible gives testimony to the truth that our actions are indispensable in the accomplishment of God's will, not because God could not accomplish it without us, but because God chooses to accomplish it with us. We in our choices are the instruments that God uses to accomplish His will and purpose.

If we are thinking about the implications of this for our initial question about the source of suffering and evil in our world, we need to recognize that none of this makes God the author of sin. Sin by definition is any act that is contrary to the will of God; and God, of course, cannot act contrary to His own will. However, as creatures made in His image with genuine choices, you and I may choose to act in opposition to God's intended will, making us the author of sin, not God. But here is where the wonder and beauty of His sovereignty appears. Even our sin, even our evil choices ultimately serve His good ends. How He does this is beyond our comprehension. That He does it is undeniable.

All of this has tremendously important implications for us. In the first place, there is no escaping the consequences of our sins. We will not "get away with" our evil acts. We cannot escape the attention of a sovereign God. He is not too busy or distracted to deal with our sins, nor is He incapable of responding to our sins as He has warned us that He will. At the same time, our sins do not thwart His plan. As the Confession points out, He may use sin in our lives "to chastise" us (V.V), as we all know from experience; He may use our sin to help us see "the hidden strength of corruption and deceitfulness of [our] hearts, that [we] may be humbled; and, to raise [us] to a more close and constant dependence for [our] support upon himself, and to make [us] more watchful against all future occasions of sin" (V.V). Those are some of the ways in which the Westminster Confession acknowledges that God uses sin to accomplish His good will and purpose in our lives. God is using our sin toward the accomplishment of His plan on our behalf.

This understanding of God's absolute sovereignty should also be for us an incomparable source of consolation in times of grief or loss. Consider this with me: No accident, no illness, no death, no crime, no loss takes place without God's sovereign leave. In other words, as He is sovereign, such events simply may not happen to us if He does not allow it. If they do happen to us, it is because He has allowed it for His good purposes. We may not be able to see what He has in mind, but we can be assured that God in His sovereignty has it well in hand.

This is the whole story of Job. We don't know the details of why God acts the way He does, but here we are allowed a glimpse behind the scenes. What happened to Job and his family? Accident, illness, death, crime, and loss all occurred to him, and they were as devastating for him as they would be for us. But we see behind the scenes, and we realize that God gave Satan leave to tempt Job with these catastrophes. At the same time God set absolute bounds on what Satan could do. God did not do evil to Job, but He allowed it in bringing about His good ends. God did not make Hitler do what he did in World War II, but He allowed it. Hitler could not have acted without God's allowance.

The suffering seems great and grievous to us, but through it God accomplishes a better and higher purpose, He assures us, than had it not taken place. The incidents are no less painful, and we don't get to see God's full purpose, but we know that God has not lost control. We see that in the story of Job. He was still protected by God. We see as we read the story that God will ultimately accomplish His good and perfect purpose in Job's life. *We* know that, although Job doesn't. But that is the great consolation of God's sovereignty, and we need to claim it in our own lives when we face adversity, when we face the unknown, when we face suffering and pain that we cannot understand.

Finally, I think there is tremendous security in knowing that God is absolutely in control of our world and of every detail of our lives. It should give us great confidence to know that no matter how great may be the threat to our welfare, our God is greater still. As Isaiah reminds us in his magnificent fortieth chapter, it is good for us to think about the God who has promised to care for us. He measures the oceans and weighs the dust of the earth. Great nations are like "a drop in a bucket," or "dust on the scales" to Him, the peoples of the earth "like grasshoppers." The earth's tyrants and noblemen, though they may seem a threat to our security, He blows away "like chaff." Indeed, His power keeps the very stars in place. Certainly this God is capable of caring for us.

It is concerning this all-seeing, all-knowing, and all-powerful God that Paul says in Romans 8:28, "And we know that in all things God works for the good of those who love him, who have been called according to his purpose." What a marvelous assurance to know that the God whose purpose cannot be thwarted has committed Himself to take every circumstance of our lives—every deliberate act and every random occurrence—and use it for the accomplishment of His ultimate good in our lives!

"What, then, shall we say in response to this?" Paul asks, considering this magnificent truth of God's sovereignty and His fatherly love for us. "If God is for us, who can be against us? . . . Who shall separate us from the love of Christ? Shall trouble or hardship or persecution or famine or nakedness or danger or sword?" (vv. 31, 35). (Note that all those things may touch our lives by God's leave, though not by His initiation.) But then he answers his own question:

> No, in all these things we are more than conquerors through him who loved us. For I am convinced that neither death nor life, neither angels nor demons, neither the present nor the future, nor any powers, neither height nor depth, nor anything else in all creation, will be able to separate us from the love of God that is in Christ Jesus our Lord. (Romans 8:37–39)

At the grand climax of His display of sovereignty in Isaiah 40, God challenges us concerning the difference this should make in our lives. How can we complain that somehow our particular concerns have escaped the attention of the God who holds the entire universe in place? "Do you not know? Have you not heard? The Lord is the everlasting God, the Creator of the ends of the earth. He will not grow tired or weary, and his understanding no one can fathom" (v. 28). You may grow weary or become discouraged about the circumstances in your life, but you are loved and cared for by a sovereign God. Can you trust Him? "Those who hope in the Lord will renew their strength. They will soar on wings like eagles; they will run and not grow weary, they will walk and not be faint" (v. 31). What a splendid privilege to serve a sovereign God!

Chapter Three

THE SHATTERED

IMAGE

Of the Nature of Humanity

Westminster Confession, chaps. IV, VI;
Ephesians 4:17–24

Meg found herself feeling profoundly frustrated once again as she left her parents' house and headed back for the apartment she shared with two of her friends. No matter how firmly she had resolved not to do it, she got into a major argument with her folks nearly every time she went home. They were so out of touch with today's world, living, it seemed, in a reactionary world of the past. This evening they had gotten into an argument about whether people were basically good or basically bad. Her father had stated in no uncertain terms that, if left to themselves, people would pretty much do the worst thing you could imagine. That, he said, is why you need police and prisons and the military. If people don't cooperate and do the right thing, you need to punish them. People don't get better by "coddling" them, he had said.

"That is so barbaric," she had argued. "Don't you know

anything about human psychology? Ninety percent of the people we lock up only get worse. People do their best when we think the best of them. The reason there are so many 'bad' people in our society is because we have abused people so consistently. If we simply start treating people better, the great majority of them will try to live up to our expectations. People generally want to do the right thing and will do it if given half a chance."

Meg's debate with her parents is not unusual. The most fundamental disagreement between a biblical view of reality and the world's view today is not, as we might anticipate, over whether God exists, or over the nature of Jesus Christ. It's not about heaven or hell, and it is not about proper moral behavior. The most critical and fundamental disagreement between Christians and the world is over how we view ourselves—the nature of humanity.

Ask people on the street whether people are basically good or basically bad, and nine times out of ten they will tell you with passionate conviction that people are basically good. But let me tell you, if that is true, we don't need the Bible and we don't need Jesus Christ! In fact, we should have a diminishing need for governments, courts, laws, and the people who enforce them.

God's Word, however, takes issue with this positive assessment of ourselves. In Genesis 6:5–6 we read, "The Lord saw how great man's wickedness on the earth had become, and that every inclination of the thoughts of his heart was only evil all the time. The Lord was grieved that he had made man on the earth, and his heart was filled with pain." "The heart is deceitful above all things," the prophet Jeremiah observes, "and *beyond cure*" (17:9). "Desperately corrupt" is the more vivid image in the RSV.

Even Jesus, who had great compassion for sinners and strugglers, would have had little patience with today's "victim mentality." He said it isn't what comes from the outside that contaminates you; it's not your parents or your society. "For from *within,* out of men's hearts, come evil thoughts, sexual immorality, theft, murder, adultery, greed, malice, deceit, lewdness, envy, slander, arrogance and folly. All these evils come from *inside* and make a man 'unclean'" (Mark 7:21–23, italics added). And the apostle Paul, quoting from the Psalms, concludes, "There is no one who does good, not even one."

"But wait a minute," you say. "That's a little harsh, isn't it? There are a lot of good people out there. Even if nobody's perfect, the number of folks who commit heinous crimes is really only a small percentage of the population. Most people live decent, respectable lives, and a few rise to truly noble acts. If we believe in people and think the best of them, most folks will live up to our expectations. A lot of antisocial behavior comes from people who have been told all their lives that they are worthless. The sort of negative things you are saying about people is really not helpful."

Two Fundamental Truths

I agree with the basic wisdom in that observation, but I would not be too quick to dismiss what God's Word tells us about ourselves. What the Bible really says goes much deeper than our casual observations. In fact, it addresses brilliantly the paradox we must admit between our human potential for great good and our simultaneous potential for unconscionable evil. The Bible reveals two fundamental truths that the world rejects, but that alone make sense of the contradictions we see in human nature. Both must be taken into account if we are to understand who we are. The two truths are these:

1. *You and I were created in the image of God.* The implications of this first truth are staggering! But . . .

2. *That image has been shattered by our intentional sin.* We must consider seriously the far-reaching implications of this truth as well.

On these two truths hang everything we know about ourselves. And only the two considered together make any real sense, or offer us any real hope, in our contradictory world.

WE WERE CREATED IN GOD'S IMAGE

Let's look at the first, the truth that we are created in God's own image. The story of creation in Genesis 1 climaxes with this account:

> Then God said, "Let us make man in our image, in our likeness, and let them rule over the [earth]." . . . So God created man in his own image . . . male and female he created them. [And] God blessed them and said to them, "Be fruitful and increase in number; fill the earth and subdue it." (vv. 26–28)

Then the account concludes, "God saw all that he had made, and it was very good" (v. 31).

Throughout the Scriptures, we hear an expression of awe concerning the human race, "fearfully and wonderfully made"; known, loved, and defended by God; given a place, according to Psalm 8:5, only slightly lower than the heavenly beings. Think about the privilege this represents! To be created in God's image implies that we are unique among all creation, that we have been singled out by God. It means that in some way we are actually like the Lord and Creator of the universe.

The biblical account leaves no doubt that we are the pinnacle of God's creation, the climax of His creative work. After He was finished creating us, He rested. Humanity was the culmination of His creation. Indeed, this picture of the human race far supersedes anything modern man thinks about himself.

Aware only that we have a larger brain than other animals and must be the product of a more sophisticated evolution, modern humans still have no particular reason for an elevated view of our worth. They may argue that we are not evil, but they have no basis on which to say that we are really good for anything either. At best they end with an innocuous view of the human race that carries no real drama or substance. At worst they have no way to distinguish us from the rest of animal life and thus no reason to consider us any more valuable than a snail. Surprisingly they may even fault us for exercising our "evolutionary advantage" at the expense of other beings.

The remarkable thing about the Christian view of humanity is that it tells us not only how low we can fall, but also how high we can rise—both lower and higher than the world acknowledges. Thus we may have a more realistic view of ourselves, as well as a more hopeful view. In the first place, we will recognize the dignity and value of all human life. That value is not gained by virtue of particular accomplishments or innate skills. We don't give value only to people who succeed or can do something better than anyone else. In the Christian view, every human being, no matter how bright or how beautiful or how skilled, has value simply because he or she is a work of art! God has made every one of us, and God doesn't make junk. He makes things that are beautiful, and He makes them on purpose. Because we view the value of human life in this way, we simply cannot take the life of an unborn baby, or a mentally handicapped child, or a depressed senior citizen, because human life is not ours to take. Each is an infinitely valuable creation of God, and we know we must be accountable for our lives and those of others. There can be no compromise in this regard.

So what does this phrase really mean: "created in the image of God"? Obviously it is terribly important. The Westminster Confession explains, "After God had made all other creatures, he created man, male and female, with reasonable and immortal souls, endued with knowledge, righteousness, and true holiness, after his own image; having the law of God written in their hearts, and power to fulfil it: and yet under a possibility of transgressing, being left to the liberty of their own will" (IV.II).

This is an enormously significant statement that is well worth exploring. We notice in this list a number of traits that identify us as human beings: reason, for example, and the possession of an immortal soul; perhaps conscience (the law of God written on our hearts); and a free will encompassing both the ability to obey and the possibility of disobedience. But does the image of God in us simply consist of our humanness, or is there something more to it? Some aspects of our humanness, after all, are quite unlike God. We have some real limitations in time and space, for example. And of course God is incapable of disobedience, nor can He be troubled by that discrepancy between what we know and what we do, which you and I call conscience.

The passage from the Confession just quoted acknowledges our humanness, first of all, but then states specifically that this rational human creature is "endued with knowledge, righteousness, and true holiness, after [God's] own image." I have come to believe that although there are many intentional parallels between the person of God and the persons He has created us to be, the actual *image of God* in us consists exclusively of our moral actions and attitudes, *our capacity for moral conduct.* God has given us *knowledge,* which is necessary in order for us to be accountable for our actions. He has also given us the potential for *righteousness* and *true holiness,* which describe conduct and attitudes that are in step with God's will. The rest of the traits that constitute our humanness —rationality, language, emotions, creativity, the abilities to choose and to communicate—are simply the means by which we are enabled to reflect the image of God.

This, then, is what we mean when we say that human beings, alone of all creation, were designed to reflect the image of God. Although it requires our unique human traits to express it, the actual image of God consists of goodness and true holiness—our stunning ability to perform acts of true courage and nobility, of compassion and grace. This being the case, we need not trouble ourselves with the many similarities between ourselves and animals. The degree to which our intelligence, for example, or our ability with language supersedes that of "lower" animals is irrelevant, for this is not essentially what distinguishes us from them. They may be intelligent too. They may even communicate. That is no threat to us. Being made in the image of God means that we, unlike anything else in all creation, are capable of reflecting His glory!

When the Shorter Catechism says: "Man's chief end is to glorify God and to enjoy him forever," it is saying that God made us uniquely in His image with the potential to reflect His utter goodness to the world. And as this is what we are created for, it is in this way alone that we will find our true joy and fulfillment.

Of course, the very things that make it possible for us to reflect the glory of God also make it possible for us to ruin everything, for we humans have tremendous capabilities. The greater our potential for good, the greater our corresponding potential for evil if we fail to do what we ought. C. S. Lewis explored this idea in *Mere Christianity.* "A cow," he says, "cannot be very good or very bad; a dog can be both better and worse; a child better and worse still; an ordinary man, still more so; a man of genius, still more so."[1] The more intelligent or capable the being, the greater the heights to which it can rise, but also the greater the depths to which it may fall. God might have made robots who would simply follow His will mechanically, but in His desire to give our lives meaning and dignity, it was necessary for Him to give us genuine choices.

You understand, there is no nobility in an apparent act of heroism if the person could not have chosen to run away. Ironically, his courage becomes evident when we learn our hero was scared to death. His nobility lies in the fact that he had the possibility of running away, but he didn't do it. He chose, even in the face of his fear, to do the right thing. In the same way, the freedom and power God has given us to reflect His image makes it possible for us not only to reflect His true glory if we obey Him, but to wreak havoc within His creation if we choose to disobey.

THAT IMAGE HAS BEEN MARRED

We must go back to the Garden of Eden to see what became of God's experiment with this unique creature capable of reflecting His image. The one thing required to keep all that incredible potential operating for good, of course, was absolute cooperation with the Creator—a willingness on the part of mankind to obey simply because God said it. That's why God gave Adam and Eve the particular test He did. Not eating the fruit may seem trivial to us, but our evaluation misses the point. Presumably God did not forbid Adam to murder Eve because He knew Adam loved Eve and wouldn't be tempted to do that. No such natural prohibitions are involved in forbidding the fruit. If Adam obeyed, it would be solely out of respect for God's authority: "I don't know why He said that, but He's God, so I'll do it." Such an attitude allows God's character to shine through a human vessel.

As we consider this test, we must pay special attention to our own tendency to resist God's authority. What was the nature of Satan's temptation? He said to Eve, "You will be like God, knowing good and evil." You see, he was tempting our first parents to do the one thing forbidden them, the thing that alone could destroy them, namely choosing autonomy—freedom from the will and power of God. It is no coincidence that this is also our constant temptation, and that it can only bring us death. If there is one thing fundamentally true about us as human beings, it is that we are ultimately dependent creatures. We do not exist on our own; we do not live by our own will or by our own power. We are absolutely dependent for our existence on the will and power of God. Not satisfied, however, to reflect God's glory, we want to shine with our own glory, to stand in the place of God. And that is really what every sin we ever commit is all about.

But that temptation is an invitation, quite literally, to suicide. To refuse to reflect God's glory is to deny the one purpose for which we were so "fearfully and wonderfully made," and the result can only be self-annihilation. God said to Adam and Eve, "You must not eat from the tree of the knowledge of good and evil, for when you eat of it you will surely die." Of course they would die, as will we when we cut ourselves off from the source of our existence. We will have severed our lifeline. We may as well dive to the ocean floor and cut off our air hose. That is what we do in seeking to be independent of God.

It is important to note that the fundamental nature of sin is not simply some weakness or imperfection, as we like to think in making excuses for ourselves. It is not just that our system failed. It is a deliberate act of disconnecting ourselves from God—a deliberate attempt to usurp power and authority from Him. This, and not some flaw in the human design, constitutes the fundamental nature of our sin. It is here that we discover the fatal act that has undermined the whole human race. Since we were created to reflect God's image by living out His goodness, such an act of rebellion can only destroy God's image in us. And this is the consequence of our rejecting God's authority.

We have not just defaced or distorted in some way God's image of holiness in our lives; *we have shattered it.* We have taken that mirror and cast it on the rocks, and it is broken in a million pieces. This is the reason God's Word speaks so categorically about the corruption of the human race. Yes, we have tremendous potential, having been made in God's image. We have capabilities that radically supersede those of any other living creature. But in rejecting God's authority in our lives, we have utterly destroyed His image.

"By this sin," the Westminster Confession reveals, "[our first parents] fell from their original righteousness and communion with God, and so became dead in sin, and wholly defiled in all the parts and faculties of soul and body" (VI.II). Genesis 3 describes the fatal consequences of this act of rebellion. First, when Adam and Eve disobeyed God and rejected His authority in their lives, they experienced a deep and profound sense of shame. The innocent delight and joy that had characterized their lives up to that point in their spontaneous relationship to God and to each other was suddenly lost, and they wanted to cover themselves. We also lose our delight in life when we choose independence from God.

Second, they found that their wonderful, intimate communion with God had been broken. They could no longer enjoy His company "in the cool of the day . . . among the trees of the garden" (Genesis 3:8). We too lose touch with the source of all beauty and wonder and power and love.

And of course, without that communion with the Creator, they found themselves utterly incapable of reflecting His image within His creation. The man and the woman could not fulfill the roles for which they had been created, whether in nurturing new life or tending God's magnificent creation. Unwilling to accept God's judgment, they began to blame each other. They said in what has become an all too familiar refrain: Something outside me has caused my downfall, not something from the inside for which I am responsible. And the world became a place of backbiting, conflict, failure, and disorder.

Now every aspect of their lives would necessarily be corrupted, since living as they ought depended entirely upon the intimacy of their communion with God. When John Calvin spoke of fallen humanity in terms of "total depravity," he was not saying every person is now as horrible as he or she could possibly be. Earlier in this chapter we reflected on the goodness we see in ordinary people. Thankfully, this is something God in His grace has preserved in order to keep our world from becoming "hell on earth." But the terrifying truth is that you and I are capable of every sin we have ever heard of! God's grace alone has held us back. Circumstances have held us back. Pride and shame have held us back. But in rejecting God's authority we have lost touch with the one source that can finally keep us from sin.

John Calvin and the Westminster Confession are saying that every aspect of who we are has now been corrupted. Nothing is left untouched. We have cut ourselves off from the God who had previously upheld and nurtured us. Our minds, designed to understand and appreciate what God was doing, are no longer capable of this sort of discernment. Our bodies, with all our marvelous capacities, from intellect to emotions to senses to will, are no longer capable of expressing true holiness. Everything intended to give our lives beauty and meaning was stripped away in that one act of rebellion in which we rejected our Source, and the result is that God's spectacular image in us has been shattered.

And ultimately, as God had warned, such a detachment from the source of life must lead to death. Our first parents began immediately to experience the corruption that would lead to death, as all the resources that had previously brought life to them had been removed.

What we see today, then (and what causes such confusion if we do not understand), is a world full of people who, first of all, have tremendous capabilities because they have been made in the image of God. Yet our disappointment comes when we realize that even though we have unimaginable powers, we have lost the ability to live up to our potential. Detached from God, our awesome capabilities only complicate our lives and deepen our malaise.

That is the bad news, but as we continue through the epic story of the human race explained by the Westminster Confession, we shall discover the overwhelming good news. God does not abandon us to our ignorance, our hardness of heart, our rebellion, and our death. Rather, He has set in motion a plan to redeem His fallen prize and restore His image in us. And He alone can do it—can pick up the million shattered pieces of His image and put them back together!

NOTE

1. C. S. Lewis, *Mere Christianity* (New York: Macmillan, 1958), 38.

Chapter Four

RECLAIMING A

BROKEN WORLD

Of Predestination (God's Initiative)

Westminster Confession, chaps. III–V;
Romans 8:28–39

*K*elsey leaned back in the stiff vinyl chair, sighed deeply, and closed her eyes. The faintly nauseating smell of catheters and disinfectants wafted over her once again. As she listened to her father's labored breathing, she realized that the knot in her stomach had not gone away for two days. It was hard to believe that the frail-looking figure in the bed next to her was really her dad, the man who had taught her how to fish, how to tune her car, and how to hold her head up when everything around her was falling apart. She was his only child, and he had been so proud of her when she got her degree from law school. They had always been close, but after her mother's death, they had become even closer.

The one thing they didn't share was her faith. She had become a Christian in college, and Christ had transformed her life, but although her father always said, "That's just great,

Kelsey. I'm proud of you," he never considered his own need for the Lord. Now here he was, barely clinging to life, and she couldn't bear the thought that he might go out into eternity with no hope of salvation. It was so frustrating. They had always talked about everything, but trying to talk to him about Jesus Christ was like talking to a lamppost. He wouldn't listen. He simply wouldn't take it seriously.

"It's hopeless if God doesn't do some sort of miracle in his life," she had finally concluded. "But how can I get God to do that? He doesn't seem interested in helping me out here at all!" The question had taken her back with a vague sense of apprehension to the book of Romans, where just this evening she had read that awful passage where God said about Isaac's twin sons, Jacob and Esau, "Before the twins were born or had done anything good or bad—in order that God's purpose in election might stand: not by works but by him who calls—she was told, 'The older will serve the younger.' Just as it is written: 'Jacob I loved, but Esau I hated.' . . . 'I will have mercy on whom I have mercy, and I will have compassion on whom I have compassion.' It does not, therefore, depend on man's desire or effort, but on God's mercy" (Romans 9:11–13, 15).

So how could she fight divine fate? God was going to do with her father whatever He desired to do. But it just didn't seem fair! Nor did it seem like the God of compassion she had come to know in Jesus Christ.

What Kelsey had run across was the foundation for the Reformed doctrine of predestination (chapter III of the Westminster Confession)—a rather horrifying doctrine that sounded to her somewhat like a congenital disease. Though she didn't really understand it, she shared the common impression that it was a statement of the rather repulsive idea that God simply chooses some people and sends them to heaven while He consigns others to hell, and there's really not much we can do about it.

Whatever we think about it, however, it is stated quite clearly in the Bible, and it won't go away just because we don't like it or we ignore it. More importantly, serious students consistently find that the most difficult teachings in the Bible often prove to be the most rewarding. So it's worth examining more closely.

I said in chapter 2 that all theology (Reformed theology insists upon this) must begin with the acknowledgment that God is absolutely sovereign. In other words, as the God of Creation, He is in absolute control of the universe, and nothing happens that is outside His control. This, of course, is a terribly important doctrine, as you can imagine. If God is not sovereign, then there are a thousand ways every day that the world might spin out of control, and we can have no assurance that things will work out all right in the end. If God *is* in complete control, by contrast, then we may be assured that everything will work out just as He planned.

RESOLVING COMPETING TRUTHS

Of course this introduces us to a serious problem in the world as we know it. If God is in absolute control of the universe, then do we really have free choice? Conversely, if we really have free choice, can God actually be in control? It is a serious dilemma! Neither option represents a universe I would like to live in. If our choices are free of God's control, then a Hitler can step in and destroy the people God has promised to protect or trigger a biological weapon that annihilates all life on the earth. On the other hand, if our choices are not free, if they are determined by God, then it would seem that we are simply God's puppets, dancing on the end of a string, and we can have no moral accountability for our actions. Indeed, if this is the case, a larger problem is introduced, for God Himself would have to be seen as the author of evil.

It would seem that we must choose one or the other. The Westminster Confession, however, embraces both. "God, from all eternity," it says, "did, by the most wise and holy counsel of his will, freely, and unchangeably ordain whatsoever comes to pass: yet so, as thereby neither is God the author of sin, nor is violence offered to the will of the creatures; nor is the liberty or contingency of second causes taken away, but rather established" (III.I). This is saying that while God determined from the beginning exactly what would come to pass in the world He created, He did it in such a way that His creatures could still make all their own choices. "Second causes" are events or actions attributable to agents other than God. "Liberty," of course, is another word for freedom, and "contingent" implies that an action was not compelled, and was therefore free from necessity. In other words, it seems to be saying that we actually can have the best of both worlds. God can be in control without taking away our free choices.

But how can that be? From what we have learned so far, free choice is fundamental to the definition of a human being. It is in our moral choices, we learned in chapter 3, that we reflect the glory of God, as we were created in His image to do. But *how can a person be a free and responsible agent if his actions have been predetermined from eternity?* We cannot be held responsible for our actions, either good or bad, if we have been compelled to them against our own will or desire. Wouldn't God's sovereign control require Him to intervene at least on occasion and compel us to act in certain ways if He is to accomplish His purpose?

Without attempting an explanation, the Scriptures simply indicate that in the midst of an impossibly complicated universe, the same God who has ordained all events has ordained human liberty, and that this liberty, while it is real, cannot challenge His sovereignty.

We are not without analogies in this difficult matter. A building contractor, for example, determines to build a particular structure. He does not do it by himself, however. After drawing up his plans, he hires scores, perhaps hundreds, of laborers, carpenters, bricklayers, painters, glaziers, interior decorators, landscapers, and others. By offering certain rewards and penalties, he coordinates all their free choices in the accomplishment of his purpose. His will is done without violating the free will of those who are his agents in the project.

But although that is a helpful analogy, any contractor would be quick to point out that a fair amount of coercion has to take place in order to assure the outcome. Not everything comes out just the way he wants. And all the while there is the possibility that someone could sabotage the entire project. Let's look at another aspect of the same question, then: *How can there be absolute certainty of what we will do if our choices are truly free?*

This requires some careful thought, but it exposes a truth that is enlightening. To say that an action is "free" is not to say that it is "uncaused." In fact, the only truly free actions are wholly determined! They are done entirely on purpose. That is why we call them "free." We did what we wanted to do. No freedom is expressed in an action that "just happens" randomly without any intent or purpose. All truly free actions have discernible causes. The question we are really asking is whether we cause an action ourselves or whether it is caused by some outside force. If we cause it ourselves, how can God be absolutely certain of the outcome of history? Has He not lost some measure of control?

FREELY CHOSEN, PERSONAL ACTIONS

Our mistake is in thinking that an action we have freely chosen cannot be certain. But of course it can be certain if we understand all the underlying causes. You can be absolutely certain, for example, that if a child you are caring for falls and splits his scalp, you will attend to the wound and try to comfort the child. No one is forcing you to do this. Yet your response is certain. Your action is freely chosen by you on the basis of who you are and what you value. Anyone who knows this about you can predict your action with absolute certainty.

For all the actions of free human agents, the causes lie deep within the character of the person acting. We act in harmony with our self-image, our values, the limits of our knowledge, our physical abilities, and the cumulative effect of all our previous thoughts, experiences, judgments, inclinations, and desires. This does not make us automatons. Quite the contrary, these are the forces that free us to act in a very specific and personal way. Because the interplay of all these factors is so tremendously complex, we may not understand why we do what we do, but clearly a sovereign God would be quite capable of understanding all of those forces, including the subtle differences in mood or circumstance that explain our inconsistency from day to day or moment to moment. And God's Word suggests that He has known this and taken it into account in the establishment of His plan for eternity. This does not mean that we *could not* have acted differently. It means only that from God's standpoint it was certain that we *would not* act differently.

As the Westminster Confession points out, this is more than foreknowledge. He, after all, created all things and has orchestrated all things for the accomplishment of His perfect will and purpose. You can't foreknow something unless it is certain, and it isn't certain unless God has determined all the factors that bring it about.

Did God then "cause" us to act as we do? Well, yes, in the sense that He created us knowing we would act completely consistently with the persons we are. That consistency, after all, renders all our free actions certain. In addition, He may often bring certain influences to bear in our lives, even as a parent may encourage a child's interest in sports or music. However, He never compels us to act in any particular way. We are never manipulated or coerced. We choose all our own actions freely. Do you begin to see how God, with His infinite knowledge and power and wisdom, can allow us to choose freely without ever losing control of any detail of life or the universe? It is indeed a magnificent concept!

Anyone who writes or reads good books will have a ready analogy for this idea. In a *good,* well-written novel, once the author has created the characters, they take on a life of their own. They may well do things that in a real sense the author never intended. But as the plot develops, each individual character must be true to himself or herself. The author is not free to break character without ruining the credibility of his book. If he writes well, we have no sense of manipulation, but a satisfaction rather that each character has acted freely and consistently with his or her own character in contributing to the final denouement. Yet that conclusion was all the time in the hands of the author. The author did precisely what he set out to do.

In much the same way, we who are characters in God's story make entirely free choices that lead *inevitably* to the accomplishment of His sovereign purposes. He, after all, is writing the book, and He is going to write the final page. We have no sense of being manipulated. We have chosen freely, and we bear the consequences of our choices, while the Author makes all things work together for the accomplishment of His good ends. "And we know that in all things God works for the good of those who love him, who have been called according to his purpose. For those God foreknew he also predestined to be conformed to the likeness of his Son" (Romans 8:28–29a). This is the great and beautiful mystery of God's sovereign will: that while His decree *guarantees* its result (Isaiah 55:11), nevertheless it *does not compel* the particular actions of free creatures. Our free choices are simply the agents of His will.

"You intended to harm me," Joseph clarified to the brothers who sold him into slavery, "but God intended it for good to accomplish what is now being done, the saving of many lives" (Genesis 50:20). Peter and John explained in Acts 4:28 that when a whole group of people, including Herod and Pilate, conspired to kill Jesus, "They did what your power and will had decided beforehand should happen." They acted with free will—but they did what God had decided beforehand would happen. Indeed, Peter and John revealed this to Jesus' murderers: "This man was handed over to you by God's set purpose and foreknowledge; and you, with the help of wicked men, put him to death" (Acts 2:23). But then they explained, "This is how God fulfilled what he had foretold through all the prophets" (Acts 3:18). There is a sense that everything is working out in every detail just as God had planned it. All the while each individual is acting with complete freedom.

THE ORIGIN OF EVIL

Perhaps we understand better the apparent contradiction between God's sovereignty and mankind's free will. But this brings us back to the problem of sin and evil in our world. Maybe you can see how sin has been allowed in our world without God being the cause. We are the cause. But God has never lost control and has even used our sin to accomplish His purpose of revealing His glory and preparing for our ultimate good.

The problem is not where sin comes from, but the devastating nature of its effect upon those of us who were created in God's image. Recall what we said about God's image in chapter 3. As we pointed out, the fundamental nature of sin is choosing autonomy from God over submission to His will. The moment we do that, for all practical purposes we are dead. We have cut ourselves off from the Source of life. The image of God in us is shattered. We had tremendous capabilities that would have enabled us to reflect the glory of God, but now we can only reflect our own broken selves. We become absolute slaves to our own corrupted nature. The apostle Paul speaks of this in vivid terms in Romans 6. It is a slavery that inevitably leads deeper and deeper into corruption until it ends in death, and we are slaves to this sin.

But the greatest problem—a very personal problem that makes predestination absolutely indispensable for us —is that once we have fallen away from God, we do not have within us the capacity to come back to Him. Paul struggled with this in that memorable passage in Romans 7 where he talked about being unable to stop sinning no matter how much he desired to do so. He was unable to return to God no matter how much effort he expended. But remember, according to those verses about Jacob and Esau with which our friend Kelsey was struggling, in the end it has nothing to do with either our effort or our desire. It has only to do with God's mercy. When Paul cried out at the end of Romans 7, "Who will rescue me from this body of death?" he introduced the whole reason for this doctrine of predestination.

PREDESTINATION AND GOD'S MERCY

Predestination is simply God taking the initiative to rescue us from this body of death. Don't ever discard this wonderful doctrine. It is our only hope! It reminds me of a fantastic but true story of a young skydiver who collided with another jumper as she leaped from the plane, and was knocked unconscious. Hurtling earthward with no way to deploy her parachute, she was bound for certain death. She could not save herself. But her instructor, a veteran skydiver, seeing her dilemma, maneuvered through the air currents until he caught up with her. With only seconds to spare, he deployed her parachute and saved her life. This is the sort of rescue every sinner requires. It is necessary because we are absolutely incapable of doing it in our own strength. So God, in His infinite love for us, chose to rescue us and give life to our lifeless hearts, with the goal of restoring His image in us and allowing us to find the joy for which we were created.

Sin has alienated us from God, but in predestination, God rolled up His sleeves, if you will, and waded in to His corrupted creation to redeem His fallen children. As I considered this difficult doctrine, an image developed in my mind of a huge mass of people fleeing down a slope and plunging into a giant cesspool in a determined effort to escape from God, glancing back from time to time in fearful defiance as they dart to and fro in an attempt to evade His grasp. But God nonetheless stands patiently grasping first one, then another, and another (we have no idea how many He will rescue in the end), plucking them out of the mass of people hell-bent on self-destruction, gently cleaning off the awful pollution of their souls, holding them to His breast, and saying, "Please stop running from Me. I love you!"

He is under no obligation to save any, of course. Since all of us have freely chosen to reject His authority, He is entirely just in condemning any or all of us to eternal death. He could never be faulted for that. Indeed, we commend a judge who condemns the guilty. Yet in His sovereign love, and in His purpose to reflect His glory within His creation, He redeems those He has chosen, though they in no way deserve it. And as this is His sovereign will, He will allow nothing to stand in His way. His plan cannot be thwarted. "Those he predestined, he also called; those he called, he also justified; those he justified, he also glorified" (Romans 8:30), conforming them to the likeness of His Son. Nothing can stand in the way of God's accomplishment of His good purpose with those He has chosen.

The difficult question for us, of course, is why He chooses one and not another. We think He should choose all or none. It may well be necessary that God's glory cannot be demonstrated in salvation if the condemnation from which we are being saved does not exist. So it may be necessary that some are condemned. But in any case, it should be comforting to note that we never see God acting arbitrarily in the Scriptures, and He certainly does not indicate here that He is acting arbitrarily, only that it is His choice. He doesn't say there are no reasons; He simply says it is His choice and He has a right to choose. We do not know why God chooses as He does, why He chose Jacob and not Esau, though part of trusting Him means trusting that when we finally see Him face-to-face, it will make perfect sense to us.

I would like to make a further observation, although, as the apostle Paul would say, this is my word, not God's. It may or may not be true, but it makes some sense. It is conceivable that He rescues only those who would, subsequent to their rescue, appreciate it and freely honor Him for it. There are, after all, people who would rather go to hell than submit to God. I do not know that this is the reason for God's choice, or even whether He needs a reason. I only know this is what He does, and I am slowly learning to trust Him.

What *is* clear, however, is that God's initiative in predestination is a priceless gift. It assures us of a *peace* with God we did not deserve. It gives us a tremendous sense of *security* to know that our salvation does not depend upon our very uncertain obedience, but only upon His certain grace. It gives us *patience* to allow the slow but certain outworking of His will in our world and *courage* to launch out boldly to do whatever He has called us to do in the power of His indwelling Spirit, knowing that He will accomplish His purpose.

What it does *not* do is encourage us to sit around and wait passively for our fate to befall us, for we have learned that our free choices and actions are precisely the tools God uses in the accomplishment of His will and purpose. The fundamental criticism of predestination is that it leads us to the conclusion that no matter what we do, God is going to do whatever He wills. But this is absolutely untrue. God says in predestination that He works through our free choices. We are the tools that God uses in the accomplishment of His will and purpose.

If, like the struggling daughter in our opening illustration, we know someone who needs God's intervention in order to save body or soul, we may confidently invest all available resources in that effort, knowing that God intends to use our efforts. We will share with the person whatever words or resources we think might be helpful. We will freely choose to pray diligently for him, knowing God has told us that He desires to use our prayers in the accomplishment of His will. And we will be *confident* in this, knowing that God does *not* act arbitrarily. He uses our prayers, He uses our self-discipline, He uses every effort at faithfulness in the accomplishment of His grand design. Through us and, yes, at times, in spite of us, He will do what is ultimately *good!*

And that is the God we are called to serve.

Chapter Five

THE

ESSENTIAL LINK

Of Christ the Mediator

Westminster Confession, chaps. VII, VIII;
Hebrews 1, 2, 4, 7, 9

*I*t was 2:00 A.M. when Phil finally flicked off the cable TV in his hotel room and sat back against the headboard of his bed. Then suddenly he slammed his fist into the pillow beside him. "I've done it again!" he muttered. "Now those images are going to plague me all week." Phil had a great job as Western regional sales manager for his firm, but it meant he had to be on the road a lot—away from his family and living in hotels. Back home he was happily married to the woman he had set his sights on when he first saw her in his English Lit class in college. They had two great kids, and two years ago Phil had become an elder in his church.

But when he was away on these trips, without his support community, he found himself doing things that really made him feel polluted on the inside. The easy access to soft-core porn movies in anonymous hotel rooms had awakened old lusts in him—lusts he thought he had left behind when he got married and especially when he started several years ago to take his faith seriously. But instead, things seemed to be getting worse. The temptations, if anything, were stronger now than ever, and had begun to spread into other areas of his life.

Regularly he confessed his sin to the Lord and vowed to do better, but no matter how often he promised, sooner or later he failed again. He had seriously begun to wonder if God would continue to forgive him for his repeated failures. And at times he found himself questioning whether he was really a Christian at all.

"Does anything really change when you become a Christian," he wondered, "or is this just one more set of good intentions that most of us are incapable of fulfilling? How is Christianity any different from any other religion or philosophy that tells us what we ought to do, but leaves us without the power to do it?"

Phil's experience, unfortunately, is not unique, and his questions are legitimate. We begin to wonder how long God will continue to forgive us if we make no progress with our sin. Is there any escape from those sins to which we become so addicted? What *does* set Christianity apart from other religions and philosophies? Does it offer anything more than another list of things we *ought* to do? Just about everybody knows how we *ought* to act. That's not our problem. Our problem is we lack the power to do it!

The Westminster Confession puts its finger on the real issue when it acknowledges that "the distance between God and the creature is so great, that although reasonable creatures do owe obedience unto him as their Creator, yet [they are unable to do it without his help]" (VII.I). "Man, by his fall," the Confession goes on to say,

". . . made himself uncapable of life by [the covenant of works]" (VII.III). You see, we are simply incapable; we don't have the resources in ourselves to obey God.

But God did not abandon us here. Instead, the Confession tells us, He introduced a new covenant. We failed to do what the old covenant (the covenant of works) required, so God introduced a covenant of grace. But we must be careful to define our terms here. When we speak of a covenant of grace, many people think it means God has given up on expecting us to do what we ought to do. He has decided to be gracious and "let us off the hook." But God's Word makes it quite clear that He does not intend only to forgive us and overlook our sins. Rather, the goal of this new covenant, the covenant of grace, is a people who are both willing and able to believe and to obey. God has no intention of accepting failure and leaving the shards of His broken creation scattered across the landscape. He intends to make all things new!

And the key to this new covenant that absolutely guarantees its success is the individual whom God has named as its mediator. Make no mistake, what distinguishes Christianity from any other religion or philosophy at any time or place in history is the person of Jesus Christ! The unique role of Jesus Christ gives Christianity its distinctive power and makes it the only approach to life that can ultimately succeed. Indeed, it is the person of Jesus Christ that makes Christianity so exciting. Let me explain.

THE PERSON OF CHRIST

What is utterly unique about Jesus Christ that He is at once fully God and fully man. He is the only person in history about whom this claim can be made. Other religions have gods and great men or women; some even claim to have men who became gods. But Jesus Christ alone combines, as the Westminster Confession says, "two whole, perfect, and distinct natures, the Godhead and the manhood, . . . inseparably joined together in one person" (VIII.II). The idea of two natures in one person is not as impossible to conceive as it may at first seem. Let's take a closer look.

First of all, Jesus Christ is fully God. The gospel of John begins by introducing us to the concept of the "Word" (*logos* in the Greek), the fundamental principle of order and rationality in the universe. That Word, we are told, already was "in the beginning"; in other words, it is eternal. Furthermore, the Word was "with God." This implies that it is distinct from God in some way. Nevertheless the Word "was God," John says. In other words, it is legitimate to say that the Word can be completely identified with God. It shares in some way the very essence of the original being.

At this point in John's gospel, the personal pronoun "he" is introduced—"He was in the beginning with God." In other words, this Word is more than a force or an idea, it is a person—who, we are told, participated in creation itself and ultimately invested that creation with life. Then, in the climax of the passage, John reveals that "the Word became flesh" and came to live within His own creation, and that Word is identified as Jesus Christ.

Introducing Jesus to the Colossian church, the apostle Paul reveals about this spectacular and unique Man: "He is the image of the invisible God, the firstborn over all creation. For by him all things were created. . . . He is before all things, and in him all things hold together"

(Colossians 1:15–17). Those are surely characteristics belonging only to God. Paul explains in that wonderful passage, Colossians 2:9, "For in Christ all the fullness of the Deity lives in bodily form." The writer to the Hebrews describes Him as "the radiance [that is, the visible reflection] of God's glory and the exact representation of his being" (1:3)—His essence, His nature. In other words, Jesus reflects the very essence of God.

We will never understand Christianity until we understand the Trinity. And although the Trinity takes us beyond our own limited perception, it is really not so difficult to understand as we often make it. To understand the Trinity, we must understand the two basic terms that are regularly used to describe it. Those words are *nature* and *person*. Let me give a simple illustration that may help you grasp the essential difference between nature and person.[1]

When I was a boy growing up in a rural community, I loved sleeping out and listening to bullfrogs serenade us all through the night. One of my favorite summer pastimes was catching frogs. Suppose one day you had come upon me and one of my friends on our bellies by a small pond, each with a large bullfrog clutched in his hands. Granting that we may be partially covered with mud and pond scum, it would not really be too difficult for you to tell the difference between us and the frogs. A biologist dissecting our amphibious friends in the lab would show you in how many ways we are alike, but there is a very fundamental difference between us, and it has to do with this thing called *nature*. My friend and I each share human nature, and the frogs share the nature of a frog. Certain characteristics that define our nature are inherent in each of us, and we can quite easily distinguish representatives of each type of being. In fact, we could do this even if we and the frogs looked alike.

More difficult, but far from impossible, is the task of telling me and my friend apart, because both of us share the nature of a human being. However, we are still separate *persons,* our second word. Even if we happen to be identical twins, indistinguishable from each other on the surface, if you get to know us you will eventually be able to tell us apart, because as individual persons we have different interests, different ways of looking at things, and different ways of responding. Human *nature* is the common set of characteristics that distinguishes us from other species, but our *personhood* is very specific. It distinguishes us from each other. Knowing how to use these two words is critical to understanding the Trinity.

THE NATURE OF THE TRINITY

Christian creeds consistently describe "one God in three persons," that is, one divine *nature,* but three individual *persons,* all of whom share that one divine nature. The persons are, of course, the Father, the Son (Jesus Christ), and the Holy Spirit. I will grant you that at first glance, this sounds like three different gods, but it is not. And the reason has to do with the uniqueness of the divine nature that they share. You see, unlike human beings who can individually reflect only a limited portion of the human essence, all three members of the Godhead share fully and completely the entire divine *nature.* Remember that the nature of a being is its essence: its inherent character or basic constitution.

It is at least as easy to distinguish God from a human

being as to tell a human from a frog, because of the differences in our nature or character. But fundamental to the essence of God is that *His* nature is indivisible. You cannot divide it up into parts. If it could be divided into various parts, God would not be whole or complete. And of course if He were not whole or complete, by definition He would not be God. So God has one, undivided nature.

Person is another matter. Personhood involves the way each of us *expresses* his or her essential nature. And while each member of the Godhead reflects the entirety of the divine nature, there is absolutely no reason God may not *express* this essential nature in several different ways. He does this through the person of the Father, who is the source and ruler of all things; the person of the Son, who is the redeemer of all things; and the person of the Holy Spirit, who communicates and applies God's truth to our lives. What is unique to the Trinity of persons who reveal the essential character of God is that, as they share one nature, they have one mind and one will. This is quite unlike individual human beings, each with our own individual minds and wills. Because they have one mind and one will, the members of the Trinity always act in complete and total concert with one another. It is impossible that they might ever contradict each other.

This, then, is the first thing we must understand about Jesus. Although He is a distinct person with a particular role, nevertheless Scripture insists everywhere that He shares fully this indivisible nature of God.

At the same time, the Bible consistently claims that Jesus is fully man. "The Word," John told us, "became flesh" (John 1:14). This truth is most fully stated in that memorable passage from Philippians 2, "[Christ Jesus] being in very *nature* God, did not consider equality with God something to be grasped, but made himself nothing, taking the very *nature* of a servant, being made in human likeness" (vv. 6–7, italics added). Notice the dual use of the word *nature.*

Here is the utterly unique thing about Jesus Christ. Though by nature God, sharing fully the essence of God, He nevertheless took upon Himself as well the nature of a human. Notice what this is and is not saying. He did not stop being God when He became a man. He was not God disguised as a person, wearing some kind of a mask, if you will. Nor did He become two persons—some sort of a schizophrenic personality. Rather, while remaining one person, now He is fully God and fully man at one and the same time.

That might seem impossible to grasp at first glance, but let's go back to our analogy for a moment. We are all familiar with the stories of the prince who, under a spell of enchantment, becomes a frog. Essential to all those stories, however, is the fact that the *person* of the prince does not simply disappear, to be replaced by a simple bullfrog. There would be no point in that. No story there. No, he is still the prince, with the mind and will of the prince, but now able to act only through the *nature* of the frog. To be true to his frog nature, he must live in a pond and catch flies with his tongue. Presumably those flies, however disgusting to him as a prince, are quite tasty to his frog palate. The trick will be for him, acting as a frog now, to accomplish whatever is necessary to end the curse. (See, you understood it all along, didn't you? You knew the story.)

That is really quite a good picture of the challenge that faced Jesus, who retained His divine nature and His distinct personhood while taking on the far more limited human nature in order to deal with the curse that now lies upon the whole human race. The Bible calls this the *incarnation*. We talk about it a lot at Christmas. It means that God has taken on human flesh as well as human nature. When the creeds declare that Jesus was "conceived by the Holy Spirit," they are stating what the angel explained to Mary in the gospel of Luke, namely that the child growing in her womb would not have an earthly father, but would be directly implanted in her by the divine Spirit, thus retaining His divine nature. It is absolutely essential, isn't it? When the creeds go on to say that Jesus was "born of the virgin Mary," they are pointing out that He received a genuine human nature from His mother. A real human nature, not a phony one. He actually carried her DNA. Fully God and fully man!

But now we begin to wonder how this works. If Jesus had both a divine nature and a human nature, would He not have two minds and two wills, since every human being, made in God's image, has his or her own mind and will? And the answer is yes! At various times, the Bible and the creeds agree, Jesus expressed Himself now through His human nature and now through His divine nature. With His divine mind, He knew Peter would find a coin in the mouth of the next fish he caught. Remember that story? But later with His human mind, He did not know when He would return to earth. Likewise in the Garden of Gethsemane, He expressed His human wish that this suffering would pass from Him, but then He submitted to the divine will instead.

Here is the key to understanding how these two natures can interact without conflict. At all times, Jesus' human nature and will were wholly subjected to His divine nature. The one *person,* Jesus, willed the same thing in both *natures.* It is like the prince acting consistently as the prince but through his frog nature. Jesus said in John 6:38, "For I have come down from heaven not to do my will but to do the will of him who sent me." This, not incidentally, should be the goal of every human being. It is the one commitment that will allow us to become the persons we were created to be. Only if our minds and wills are submitted ultimately to the nature of God may we reflect the very image and glory of God!

CHRIST, THE LINK BETWEEN GOD AND MAN

Here then we have arrived at the very heart of our study. Jesus' indispensable dual nature as fully God and fully man allows Him now to serve as the essential "link" between us and the God from whom, as we learned in chapter 3 on the Shattered Image, we have been cut off by our sin. Darwinists look for the "missing link" between human beings and the lower animals, but the really important link was on the other side, between human beings and God. As we shall see, this link is absolutely essential for our life and our salvation. Life and salvation are only found in God. If we are cut off from Him we are in serious trouble. The essential link is found in Jesus Christ.

Those verses we quoted from Philippians 2 about Jesus retaining His divine nature while taking on a human nature climax with an account of His subsequent death and exaltation. This points us to the incredible feat that Jesus set out to accomplish. The first thing He had to do as a human being was defeat the curse that had doomed the whole human race, the curse with which the man in our opening illustration was struggling and with which you and I are struggling as well. Three aspects of this curse need to be addressed: Satan, who was our primary tempter; sin, which had left us with true guilt and therefore separated us from a holy God; and death, which was the natural and eternal consequence of our sin. Let us trace Jesus' incredible accomplishment as the book of Hebrews records it.

> Since the children have flesh and blood, he too shared in their humanity so that by his death he might destroy him who holds the power of death—that is, the devil—and free those who all their lives were held in slavery by their fear of death.... For this reason he had to be made like his brothers in every way, in order that he might become a merciful and faithful high priest in service to God, and that he might make atonement for the sins of the people. (Hebrews 2:14–15, 17)

Do you see it? His death is intended to release us from bondage to Satan, sin, and death. That is His whole purpose. Satan uses the fear of death and our desire for security to tempt us to lie, to cheat, to steal, to seek personal pleasure while it is at hand and ignore the call of God to higher things. Sin becomes for us an addiction. Its insatiable appetite continues to demand satisfaction from us. Meanwhile the guilt we incur enslaves us to death unless the penalty is paid.

But Jesus, according to the unfolding story in the book of Hebrews, became our high priest. A high priest, you might remember from the Old Testament, had a very specific role. The high priest always brought a sacrifice for sin into the holy place, where he interceded on behalf of the people. He would plead for God's mercy in spite of the fact that the people had sinned. Jesus, as wholly God and wholly man, became a unique mediator with God the righteous judge on our behalf. In the first place, as Isaiah predicted and Peter explained, Jesus took all our sins upon Himself vicariously and offered Himself up as a sacrifice to pay the penalty of death incurred by our guilt. *As a man,* Jesus could identify with our sins and offer the penalty required of a human being, namely death. But *as God,* that penalty could be multiplied infinitely to cover the sins of the whole human race. Do you begin to see how important it is that He participates fully in both?

What is more, since death could not contain Him, He rose from the dead and was exalted to the right hand of God the Father. From there what does He do? The letter to the Hebrews tells us He intercedes for us. Right there at the right hand of God He pleads our case in such a way that there is no possibility that His request for mercy toward us would be denied, since His mind and will are precisely the same as those of God the Father. What an intercessor!

Then we come to the climax, in which we see that He is different from us yet simultaneously connected to us:

> Because Jesus lives forever, he has a permanent priesthood. Therefore he is able to save completely those who come to God through him, because he always lives to

88

intercede for them. Such a high priest meets our need—one who is holy, blameless, pure, set apart from sinners, exalted above the heavens. Unlike the other high priests, he does not need to offer sacrifices day after day, first for his own sins, and then for the sins of the people. He sacrificed for their sins once for all when he offered himself. (Hebrews 7:24–27)

Then comes His incalculable offer, worth reading in its entirety in Hebrews 8 and 9. He offers us the new covenant, about which we spoke at the beginning of this chapter, the covenant of grace that replaces the covenant of works at which we failed so miserably. This new covenant unites us with Jesus Christ and puts His Spirit to work within us to transform our hearts and our lives. And the key to our enjoyment of this amazing victory is our union with Jesus Christ, the union that God now offers us. In our union with Jesus Christ, the power of Satan, the power of sin, and the power of death are defeated in our lives because Jesus defeated them and we are in union with Him. Furthermore, in His resurrection, new and indestructible life is extended to us as well.

All this is possible because, although we could not be united with God in His holy and perfect nature, we *could* be united with Jesus in His human nature. So you see why the unique nature of Christ is so crucial. Having been tempted as we are, the writer to the Hebrews points out, He can sympathize with our sin, even though He Himself did not fail. But of course since Jesus, having two natures, is also in complete union with God, our union with Jesus effectively places us in union with God the Father and with His Holy Spirit as well, the absolutely indispensable link between God and us. Through

Him, we have a direct connection with the very life and power of God, a connection we, as sinners, must otherwise have been denied. Now our sin has become His sin and His death has become our death on behalf of our sin. His resurrection to new life has become our resurrection to new life. His power flows through us. All this comes about because we are in union with Jesus Christ.

Perhaps the best analogy in the Scriptures for this union with Christ, found in John 15 and Romans 11, is the picture of a branch grafted into a vine—in our case a diseased branch grafted into a healthy vine or tree. In that union, the disease of the branch is carried away, and the branch is instead invested with the life of the healthy root. And God says believers are grafted into Jesus Christ. What a special promise for those He has brought into union with Christ in His human nature—with Christ who is, in turn, related to God the Father in His divine nature.

But let's get practical. What about that man in our opening illustration? (A critical illustration because that man is so like us!) What about that man who, although he had become a Christian and was presumably in some sort of union with Jesus Christ, nevertheless experienced so little of Christ's power over sin in his life? The answer is a very practical one, and it involves a singular commitment on our part. As Jesus makes clear in John 15:4 (KJV), each branch has a responsibility to "abide in the vine." The power is there, if we prove our faith by keeping in touch with Him.

Let me give an illustration. The nature or qualities of fire and of cold steel are quite distinct and almost diametrically opposed. Nevertheless a steel sword, placed in a hot fire, will eventually become hot itself and take on the qualities of the fire. Were you to place it in water, it would cause the water to boil. You might even set wood on fire with a white-hot sword. What causes that powerful reaction? Is it the qualities of the sword or the qualities of the fire? Well, obviously it is the qualities that are inherent in the fire, not the qualities that are inherent in the sword. However, those qualities have now become the qualities of the sword. The sword is now able to accomplish what only the fire could accomplish before, and the reason is that it never left the presence of the flame.

And that is the challenge to you and me in abiding in Jesus Christ and experiencing His power in our lives. We have to abide in the power of His presence! We have to keep our sword in the flame—through worship, through prayer, through meditation on the Word, through personal discipline that continues to work out what God is working in us. It is not our efforts that overcome sin. It is not our efforts that accomplish great and wonderful things. But our efforts need to be focused simply on staying close to Jesus Christ, the mediator of this new covenant—abiding in Him, being immersed in His Spirit. If we will, His immeasurable power will be released in our lives.

NOTE

1. I am indebted to Jon E. Braun in his book *It Ain't Gonna Reign No More* (New York: Thomas Nelson, 1978) for inspiring me with the idea of how boys and frogs might illustrate person and nature.

Chapter Six

A DAY OF

RECKONING

Of Justification

Westminster Confession, chaps. IX–XI;
Romans 3:19–26

*W*hen the realization struck Arlen, it was like a cement truck going downhill. Why in the world should God forgive him for a sin he had committed absolutely on purpose? It was not an inadvertent sin—he had done it quite intentionally. It wasn't a sin of passion—it was a calculated act of deceit. In fact he had probably done the same thing a thousand times on purpose! He knew in advance it was wrong. And he knew in advance he was going to do it. There was no way his company could deliver the product in the time he had confidently assured his customer it would be done. But, he had told himself, he didn't really have a choice. If he told the truth, they would lose this account that they so desperately needed.

What he had done, however, hit him that night as he sat up in bed reading his Bible while his wife slept next to him. From Psalm 15 he had read: "Lord, who may dwell in your sanctu-

ary? Who may live on your holy hill?" *(v. 1). And the answer:
"He whose walk is blameless and who does what is righteous,
who speaks the truth from his heart . . . who keeps his oath even
when it hurts" (vv. 2–4). As he laid his Bible down in his lap
and reviewed his day in the light of those verses, he was suddenly
aware of how deceitful he had become. Jeremiah says, "The heart
is deceitful above all things, and desperately corrupt; who can
understand it?" (17:9 RSV). The worst of it is we hardly know
the deceit of our own hearts.*

As he reflected on it, Arlen recognized that he almost never
told the straight truth anymore. Everything was shaped, everything was calculated for the effect he desired. He seldom even
considered telling the truth if it would hurt his cause. The fact
was, according to God's Word, he simply did not qualify to come
into God's holy presence.

Oh, he knew his friends would laugh at him for getting all carried away with such a trivial sin. It wasn't as if he had murdered
somebody. Everybody stretched the truth now and then. But Arlen
was haunted by the realization that God was under no obligation
to forgive him. Indeed, the Old Testament sacrifices absolved only
unintentional sin (Numbers 15:27–31). For those who sinned
flagrantly or defiantly, the Bible simply warned of impending judgment (Hebrews 10:26–27). There really was no excuse for his
untruthfulness. Why should God be merciful to him? Why should
He be merciful to us when we have sinned on purpose?

In fact, as he thought about it, he began to wonder how a
just God could simply overlook or dismiss any sin the way we
do and the way we hope He will. If God wanted a perfect world
(and there was really no hope for the future if He did not), then
God had to take sin seriously—ALL sin. It occurred to Arlen
that he wasn't at all sure he wanted to live in a world where God
just let sin go. But if God did judge sin, then a day of reckoning

was certain to come for him as well, and there were a lot more sins on his list than just a few lies.

What Arlen had begun to think about was the fundamental question that underlies the doctrine of justification: How can a sinner be at peace with a holy God? If God is truly holy—embracing no imperfection at all—then how could God possibly embrace unholy men and women like you and me? It's not a matter of turning the other way and ignoring it; it's not a matter of tolerating "just a little sin." That would be like you or me accepting a blood transfusion that contained "only a little" of the AIDS virus. Either we are free from this lethal virus or we are not. Either God is utterly holy or He is not holy at all. Do you understand the problem? He *cannot* embrace us if we are unholy, and we are indeed unholy.

And this is our dilemma. It is the dilemma that nearly drove Martin Luther to despair, but which in the end, happily, inspired the Reformation. The average person may be blithely ignorant of the jeopardy in which he stands, but Luther, like the apostle Paul before him, could see the whole human race, every one of us, like a horde of lemmings plunging over a cliff into the sea. "There is no one righteous," the apostle Paul had quoted from the psalms, "not even one; there is no one who understands, no one who seeks God. All have turned away, they have together become worthless; there is no one who does good, not even one" (Romans 3:10b–11).

OUR FUNDAMENTAL NATURE

The fundamental reality of our broken world is that every one of us is *morally bankrupt*. There is no good thing in our account. We are not selfless, as we ought to be; we are fundamentally selfish. And if we have not yet recognized that about ourselves, we are in even more serious trouble than we thought. We are not yielded to God's authority in our lives; we are constantly fighting for and justifying our desire for autonomy.

In the Inquirer classes in our church, we walk through the Ten Commandments together. We learn that even if we think we are keeping God's commandments, Jesus calls our attention to our motives, and we realize that in spirit if not in practice we have broken them all. We have not only done the things we ought not to have done, but we have also failed to do the things that we ought to have done. Indeed, what we were created to do was to glorify God, and clearly we have failed to do that. The result is, according to Paul in Romans 1, that while we think we are wise, in fact our thinking has become futile and our hearts have become dark. There is no excuse for this, and we are on our way inevitably to death.

Far and away the most dangerous thing about our society today is not our acts of sin in themselves but our refusal to acknowledge our sin. The first three chapters of the book of Romans were written precisely for the purpose of convincing us that, whatever we are, we are decidedly NOT OK. That is not something we want to hear, but God's Word says if we don't start there we are in serious trouble. As much as we do not like to admit it, nothing can get better in our lives until we recognize, first of all, that we are fundamentally not the way we are supposed to be. Denying this is very much like having a cancer in your body that you refuse to acknowledge.

Nobody likes to think about it, but ignoring it or pretending it does not exist will ultimately prove fatal. The only way we can deal with that fatal disease is to acknowledge it, the sooner the better, and begin to deal with it. The Bible is telling us that every one of us harbors in our lives a moral malignancy that will destroy us if we refuse to deal with it. That is the starting point for the gospel.

Oh, we may not think we are so bad. We see others at an advanced stage of the disease, and we pride ourselves in our relative health. Other people's bodies and souls are ravaged by this ruthless enemy, but so far our symptoms have been quite mild. Listen! If there is any sin in your life whatsoever, it is evidence that the fatal disease is present in you. It may not seem serious now, but left untended *it will eventually destroy you*. That is the nature of sin, and that is what we have to understand before we even begin.

The indictment handed down against each one of us then is that we are sinners. But even worse, we are morally bankrupt. We do not have the means to extract ourselves from our predicament; we have no moral capital with which to pay our debts. We have a fatal disease, aggravated by our own choices. And the penalty each of us must suffer for our sins when the day of reckoning comes is death—the wrath of God against sin.

OUR INABILITY TO UNDERSTAND

If our first problem is our refusal to acknowledge our sin, our second problem is our inability to accept the wrath of God against sin. Since *we* don't take sin all that seriously, we don't see why God should take it all that seriously. We think God should be more tolerant. Unfortunately, the Bible shows God to be absolutely uncompromising about sin.

But if sin is in fact the fatal condition that God's Word says it is, then He had better be uncompromising about it! Would you go to an oncologist who was less than uncompromising about malignant cancer cells showing up in your body? I think you would want that doctor to be uncompromising. What would you think of a physician who just ignored the evidence of a malignancy in your body, and told you not to worry about it? Yet that is exactly what we do with our sin.

God, by contrast, is ruthless with sin. We sometimes fault Him for that, but that is His great glory. He is ruthless with sin because He knows how utterly destructive it is. There is no such thing as a harmless sin. All sin leads eventually to death. It is both the natural result of our insistence on walking away from God and the just penalty that He imposes on us for our rebellion. It has to be, for God's great goal and intent for creation is a perfect paradise that can be thoroughly enjoyed without any limitations or reservations. If He allows sin to be harbored there, the paradise is destroyed.

Many in our society talk as if tolerance is always good and intolerance is always bad. But what would you think if you went away on vacation to what was advertised as a wonderful resort overlooking a spectacular mountain lake, a place stocked with abundant supplies for rest and recreation—but when you got there you found that the manager's careless tolerance for his workers' poor performance had allowed the resort to deteriorate markedly? The pool and Jacuzzi had become contaminated and couldn't be used, facilities fairly consistently failed to work, bedrooms were not clean, and the food was often bad. I don't think you would be impressed with that manager's tolerant attitude. I think you would consider him a failure. A good manager is intolerant of poor performance.

That is what we have to understand about God as well. God cannot tolerate sin. What will not be restored by His touch must be cast away. That is why death is the ultimate penalty for our sin: It is the casting away of all who will not be healed. Death alone, separation from God, can maintain the integrity of His kingdom. It is a removal of all things polluted.

But of course the problem is that we are, all of us, infected with the fatal disease of sin. We are *all* guilty before a holy God. God could not change His reaction to our sin even if He wanted to. It is the absolute contradiction of His character. He may love us more than we can possibly imagine, but He cannot withdraw His wrath against sin. Therefore you and I must necessarily perish *unless* God can somehow spare us without violating His own holy character. That is the question—how can He spare us sinners without violating His own holiness?

Here we discover the true brilliance at the very heart of the gospel. God *does* find a way to resolve this seemingly impossible dilemma, and He does it, Romans 3:23–24 says, by *justifying* the sinner. "All have sinned and fall short of the glory of God"—in other words, none of us deserves to escape God's wrath against sin—"[but we] are justified freely by his grace through the redemption that came by Christ Jesus."

It is very important for us to understand what this word *justify* means if we are to grasp the heart of the

Christian faith. To justify does not mean to forgive. To justify does not mean to make us good. Rather to justify is to declare that we are *not guilty.* It is simply a legal declaration that in fact we bear no guilt. In the Bible (Deuteronomy 25:1), as in our society, a judge is required to *justify* the righteous and to *condemn* the guilty. These are the two sides of justice. If a judge justifies the righteous, that does not mean that he forgives them, does it? He doesn't have to; the righteous don't need to be forgiven. Nor does it mean that he makes them righteous; they already are. No, he is just *acknowledging* that they are righteous when he justifies them. And he is acknowledging that the others are guilty when he condemns them.

But if you are with me you should be lost! How in the world can God justify the wicked, which Romans 4 says He does? It is the very reason we would throw any judge off the bench! The last thing we expect of a good judge is for him to justify the wicked. Clearly, such an action would be a travesty of justice—though most of us would be happy if it were applied to *us* once we recognize our own sinfulness. How is it that a holy God can declare something to be true that He has just said unequivocally is *not true?* That's the problem that is resolved with this doctrine of justification. How can God justify someone who is in fact guilty? Well, an important clue is found in Romans 4, where the example of Abraham is lifted up for us. Abraham was far from righteous. If you trace Abraham's life through Genesis you will find that he failed again and again; but God says Abraham believed God and it was "credited" to him as righteousness (Romans 4:3). There's the clue to what God is doing in justification.

The terms Paul uses here suggest an analogy, which begins to make sense of our dilemma. What, after all, is a "day of reckoning," the title of this chapter? *Reckoning* is an accounting term. It has to do with totaling up our assets and our liabilities. The problem with a day of reckoning for us is that we are morally bankrupt. We owe a huge debt, we have a huge liability because of our sin—an insurmountable liability—and we have no assets with which to counter it. We have no righteousness in ourselves by which to offset our debts. We rightly fear a day of reckoning, because on that day we will be found guilty and worthy only of death and separation from God. The honest person recognizes this and realizes that if God doesn't do something about it, he is doomed.

GOD'S WILLINGNESS TO JUSTIFY

But God is saying in Romans 3 and 4 that He is willing to cancel our debt and even more astonishingly to credit our account with His own righteousness. The Westminster Confession says, "Those whom God effectually calleth, he also freely justifieth . . . by pardoning their sins, and by accounting and accepting their persons as righteous; not for anything wrought in them, or done by them, but for Christ's sake alone" (XI.I).

It is quite as if we had incurred an enormous financial debt that we had no means to pay. Our own account is empty. But at this point a billionaire steps forward and says, "I will credit your account with enough to pay this debt, and not only that, but so that you may afford wonderful things in addition, I will give you unlimited access to all my wealth." God says, "I will pay the debt of death for your sins. Of course you don't deserve it, but I will do it because I love you. And furthermore, so that you may afford the wonder and joy of heaven with Me, I will credit your account as well with all My righteousness."

One of the keys to unlocking the mystery of justification in the Bible is to recognize it has nothing to do with our righteousness. That is the primary cause of our confusion. We are always thinking about our own righteousness when we ask the question: Are we righteous enough to qualify for God's kingdom? And the answer is always, "No, we aren't." We never were. In fact (and here is the most surprising thing), God never expected us to be from the beginning! We were created not to reflect our own righteousness, but to reflect God's. We are incapable of righteousness in ourselves. Only as we reflect God's righteousness can we fulfill the purpose for which we were created. So now, to justify us and declare us to be righteous, God says He will have to cancel our debt and invest in us His own righteousness to accomplish the thing He set out to do at the very beginning (XI.I).

All right, but how does this happen? It is easy enough to draw the analogy of an account book, but how can God cancel my debt? The Westminster Confession says, "Christ, by his obedience and death, did fully discharge the debt of all those that are thus justified" (XI.III). But how can all this honestly apply to me? It is I who owe God goodness and truth and decency, after all, and I have not given it. Therefore I am guilty and liable to the penalty of death. For Him to "let me off" by paying my debt doesn't really seem fair when it comes down to it. Nor does it seem fair that I get credit for righteousness that is not my own.

If you recognize that, you are very close to understanding the heart of justification. It is indeed something you do not deserve. In fact, it is something you could never attain by your own efforts. If it is to be yours at all, it must be given to you as a gift. You may accept it and live within God's kingdom, or you may reject it and die alone, but those are your only options.

THE NECESSITY OF FAITH

If it is ever to be ours, however, the next thing we have to understand is faith. Faith is the means by which we appropriate the gift of justification. Faith is not just belief. Faith is trust in a particular object. Let's say you were drowning. You finally abandon hope of saving yourself and cling to a life preserver that's thrown to you from the shore. You have put your trust entirely in that object, and it becomes the source of your salvation from death by drowning. The faith we are speaking of here, of course, is a trust in the person of Jesus Christ, the mediator we discovered in the last chapter, who becomes our life preserver—our bridge over the chasm of Death— our link to Life. To trust Jesus Christ is to surrender one's life to Him. He is the One who saves, but our faith is the means of that salvation—the act of trust that makes it possible.

So trust in Jesus Christ becomes the means by which we are saved from death, but also the means by which sin is gradually overcome in our lives and we are enabled to become the people God created us to be before we fell by our sin. All this can take place because faith, as with the person clinging to the life preserver, attaches us to Jesus Christ. His thoughts become our thoughts, His will our will. We spoke briefly in the last chapter about the importance of union with Jesus Christ. It is here that we begin to see the implications of this union for our lives. The doctrine of justification depends entirely upon our union with Jesus Christ.

When we become Christians, Romans 6:5–11 explains, we become united with Jesus Christ both in His death and in His resurrection. Let me explain the significance of this with an illustration that parallels John's analogy of branches grafted into a vine. To clarify the effect on us, however, I want to change the analogy to the relationship of individual organs to the body. For the purpose of this illustration, you and I are represented by the individual organs. Suppose a fatal disease has invaded one of those organs, like the heart. The heart muscle begins to shrivel, and the heart's death is imminent. In traditional medicine, of course, the radical solution would be a heart transplant in order to save the body, and the diseased heart would be discarded. But since in this case the diseased heart itself represents us, we will need an even more radical solution.

So let us suppose that in this decidedly nontraditional approach to medicine, we reverse the process, and the fatally diseased heart is transplanted into a healthy body. What do you suppose will happen? Well, I expect that the disease will eventually take the life of the new body. But now comes the truly radical part of the solution. Suppose that this second body is raised from the dead and restored to life. What will now be the experience of the transplanted organ? Well, of course, that organ will be restored also and made whole and new—in fact made invulnerable within that new resurrected body as the life of that new body flows through the restored organ.

Strange as it may seem, this is what God does for us through the union with Christ that makes possible our justification. It involves a reverse heart transplant! We are diseased hearts, bound inevitably for destruction. But in justification God through faith places us in union with Jesus Christ. And two primary things happen as a result of that union. First of all, Jesus Christ, having taken our disease of sin into Himself, dies. He is absorbing the penalty of death for our sins. God had warned us that the wages of sin was death and this has proved to be true. But unexpectedly we have not died alone, to be discarded and forgotten. Rather we have died in Him. The unavoidable penalty of death for our sin, then, is paid through *His* death on the cross because we are in Him. That is the first step in justification—our debt is paid.

LIFE IN CHRIST

But then comes the other, more positive side of justification. As we are in union with the resurrected Christ, we are now brought back to life in Him! But this time it is not to begin our failure all over again. Now the very life and righteousness of Christ Himself flows through us, like the spirit of new life flowing through the transplanted heart: "When God converts a sinner, and translates him into the state of grace, he freeth him from his natural bondage under sin; and, by his grace alone, enables him freely to will and to do that which is spiritually good" (IX.IV). The righteousness necessary for a place in God's presence has now been supplied by the righteousness of Jesus Christ flowing through us. God finds us acceptable, *not* because of anything in us, but because of what is found in Jesus Christ. His, after all, was the only true righteousness to begin with. All God ever wanted was to see His righteousness displayed in us.

And, as a final bonus, as Christ's life flows through us, God lets us experience the delight of His own righteousness. There never was anything intrinsically good within us. We are nothing more than dust into which God has breathed life. All of our pitiful attempts at righteousness were no more than dust cloths (the Bible calls them "filthy rags") anyway. But Christ's righteousness alone restores our peace with God. And in the end, since we are grafted (or transplanted) into Jesus Christ, when He comes into the paradise of God's presence, we come as well.

And that is how God can be just, not violating His own perfect justice, and still justify those of us who deserve nothing, but have been grafted into Jesus Christ.

Let's return to the man in our opening illustration. If he has trusted Jesus Christ as the only source for his salvation, if he has recognized his own sinfulness and accepted Christ's righteousness on his behalf, then he has been united with Christ through that act of faith. His sin, therefore, has been paid for by Christ's death, and if he will confess it and repent of it, he will be forgiven. This does not give him license to sin with impunity, of course. That would contradict the whole idea of the faith that submits to Jesus Christ, seeking His righteousness. It would be like letting go of the life preserver. Forgiveness and power for living are ours only if the desire of our heart is to reflect that true righteousness. But if that is our desire and we come to Jesus Christ for it, He gives it to us in union with Him. Now finally we are free from the debt of sin, and the power of Jesus Christ in us goes to work to begin to conform us to His image.

Chapter Seven

TO BE

TRULY LOVED

Of Adoption

Westminster Confession, chap. XII;
Romans 8:12–17

here is, deep within the heart of every one of us, an irrepressible longing to be loved. In his book *Habitation of Dragons,*[1] Keith Miller relates this true story, told to his small group by a friend whose name was Alice:

When I was a tiny little girl, I was put in an orphanage. I was not pretty at all, and no one wanted me. But I can recall longing to be adopted and loved by a family as far back as I can remember. I thought about it day and night. But everything I did seemed to go wrong. I tried too hard to please everybody who came to look me over, and all I did was drive people away. Then one day the head of the orphanage told me a family was going to come and take me home with them. I was so excited, I jumped up and down and cried. The matron reminded me that I was on trial and that it might not be a permanent arrangement. But I just knew it would be. So I went with this family and started to school in their town—a very happy little girl. And life began to open for me, just a little.

But one day, a few months later, I skipped home from school and ran in the front door of the big old house we lived in. No one was at home, but there in the middle of the front hall was my battered old suitcase with my little coat thrown over it. As I stood there and looked at that suitcase, it slowly dawned on me what it meant . . . they didn't want me. And I hadn't even suspected.

Miller says, "Alice stopped speaking a moment, but we didn't notice. We were each standing in that front hall with the high ceiling, looking at the battered suitcase and trying hard not to cry. Then Alice cleared her throat and said . . . 'That happened to me seven times before I was thirteen years old.'"[2]

Most of us will never have to suffer the pain of such rejection. Our relationships with spouses or family are at least satisfactory. We know we are loved, though perhaps we are never quite secure in it. Yet we can feel something of her pain because even the best of our relationships in a fallen world disappoint us. They never seem to be quite what they promise. And the reason is that in the end every earthly relationship only suggests the relationship for which you and I were created.

Let me tell you the most incredible truth that has ever been revealed: *You and I were created to be loved by God.* It's true! We were created to be a part of His family, to have God Himself as our Father, and to enjoy the incredible privileges of His household. For reasons I do not understand (perhaps because Satan wants to hide from us the profound implications of this truth), this doctrine of adoption is the most neglected doctrine in the entire Bible. The Westminster Confession of Faith is one of the few creeds that deals with it at all, and it has only one paragraph on the subject. Yet it is the climax of the gospel story that God intended from the dawn of time to arrange that you and I might be taken into His family to enjoy the astonishing privileges of a relationship with Him.

PROGRESSION IN INTIMACY: NAMES OF GOD

As the Old Testament begins, we hear of God as *El Shaddai,* God Almighty, the powerful ruler of the universe. When God reveals His covenant name to Israel, it is *Yahweh,* "I am that I am" (Exodus 3:14 KJV), the source of all being, self-existent, sovereign, and wholly free from dependence upon anything beyond Himself. The emphasis always is on His "otherness," as we are introduced to God in the Old Testament: His holy and untouchable purity. Before this terrifying God each of us must humble ourselves and hope desperately for a mercy we know we do not deserve.

But in the New Testament, an absolutely remarkable truth emerges, one we had no right to expect. Through Jesus Christ we learn that, while God has not compromised anything of His holiness, nor released us from the need for purity and for humility before Him, yet He has given us a new name by which we who enter into covenant with Him may address Him. And that name is "Father." Indeed, as Romans 8:15 says, we can call the Holy Lord of the universe "Abba." *Abba* was an Aramaic term by which a child might address his father. The closest we come to this is our word "Papa."

This is an astonishing turn of events! God is still

utterly holy and righteous and good, and we are still sinners with entirely polluted souls. Yet far from God's
being inaccessible to us as He was in the awesome "Holy
of Holies" at the center of the Old Testament tabernacle
—a God who could only be approached once a year by
the high priest after many sacrifices—God now says that
we may approach Him boldly and naturally, through a
way opened up by Jesus Christ Himself. We might
approach Him as a child climbs into his parent's lap just
to feel the embrace of one who will never stop loving
him.

It is important to recognize, however, that this is not
true of everyone indiscriminately. To be called "children
of God" in the New Testament is a special privilege. It
does not apply to all people simply because we have been
created by God. The New Testament speaks everywhere
of two distinct families, and even two distinct father-
hoods in this world. "You belong to your father, the devil," Jesus told those who rejected Him, "and you want to
carry out your father's desire" (John 8:44). "If God were
your Father, you would love me," Jesus said (v. 42a). We
are, each of us, born into this world a natural man or a
natural woman, separated from God our true Father by
our sin. But the good news of the gospel is that God
loved us so much that He sent His "only begotten" Son
into this world to prepare a way by which we may claim
a place within His family (John 3:16 KJV).

Jesus' relationship with God the Father is unique, and
this is instructive also. Jesus is "begotten." The Bible tells
us that He is the *only* begotten Son of the Father. When
we beget something (a child) we do not gather up other
substances from which to form it. Rather it comes forth

out of our very being. When the Bible says that Jesus is God's "only-begotten son," as the Nicene Creed explains it, it means He is of one substance with the Father. He comes forth from the Father's very being. He is the Father's only "natural-born" Son, if you will. As a human child, begotten by human parents, shares fully in the human nature, so Jesus Christ, begotten of God, shares fully in the nature of God the Father. Of course these terms do not mean that Jesus only came into being at a particular point in time the way we do. John makes it clear in the introduction to his gospel that Jesus existed in the beginning with God the Father. But Jesus Himself explained in John 8:42 that He had come or "proceedeth forth" (KJV) from God. This simply means that He shares the essence that originated with God the Father. And He is alone in this.

INVITATION TO FAMILY RELATIONSHIP: ADOPTION

The Westminster Confession says of adoption:

All those that are justified, God vouchsafeth, in and for his only Son Jesus Christ, to make partakers of the grace of adoption, by which they are taken into the number, and enjoy the liberties and privileges of the children of God, have his name put upon them, receive the spirit of adoption, have access to the throne of grace with boldness, are enabled to cry, Abba, Father, are pitied, protected, provided for, and chastened by him, as by a Father: yet never cast off, but sealed to the day of redemption; and inherit the promises, as heirs of everlasting salvation. (XII.I)

"Yet to all who received him," the apostle John informs us in the first chapter of his gospel, "to those who believed in his name, he gave the right to become children of God—children born not of natural descent, nor of human decision or a husband's will, but born of God"—born because of God's initiative in reaching out to us. Here is our invitation to a place in God's family. Those who believe in the name of Jesus, and who receive Him as Savior and Lord, are *adopted* out of this alien family, a family bound for death, and transferred into the family of God Himself.

This doctrine of adoption has incredible implications for us. Most evangelicals—and by that term I mean those believers who hold to the absolute authority of God's Word and who bear witness to Jesus Christ as the only source of genuine life—tend to emphasize the doctrine of *justification* outlined in the last chapter. This is, of course, a great and fundamental truth. It is the revelation that God has dealt with the demands of the law on our behalf and now declares us "not guilty" before Him. But while it is a tremendous relief to know that the penalty for our sins has been paid, this says nothing at all about our subsequent relationship with God. He might well have said, "There, I have paid for your sins, though you didn't deserve it. But I am thoroughly disappointed with you. Now just stay out of My sight and don't trouble Me anymore with your grievous behavior."

He might have said that, but He didn't! Instead, incredibly and quite unexpectedly, He said, "Now that I have purchased your forgiveness with the blood of My only-begotten Son, I want to clothe you in His righteousness. I want to offer you a place beside Him in My family, in My kingdom. You may be My sons and daughters also, sharing fully in the rights and privileges of My household, for I want to adopt you as My own!" See what a grand image this is? This is not simply the judge setting the prisoner free, though if we are the prisoner we are happy enough to be free. This is the waiting father, rushing out to embrace his wayward son, putting the royal robe upon his shoulders, placing a ring on his finger, ordering a great feast in his honor, and restoring him to a place of wealth and privilege in his own home.

Adoption is so much more than any other part of the salvation process. It speaks of the great love of the Father, and of His commitment to spend all His resources to establish and maintain a relationship with us as His children and ultimately His heirs. It speaks of intimacy, affection, generosity, and privilege. And it speaks of a relationship that God initiated before all time, and that nothing can sever because it is the decision of a sovereign God. God is *able* to do everything He *determines* to do, and He has determined to make us His children. In Ephesians 1:4–5 we read, "For he chose us in him [Christ] before the creation of the world to be holy and blameless in his sight. In love he predestined us to be adopted as his sons through Jesus Christ, in accordance with his pleasure and will." Reflecting on this late in life, Jesus' close friend John wrote, "How great is the love the Father has lavished on us, that we should be called children of God! And that is what we are!" (1 John 3:1).

It is, of course, a more complex story than the familiar one of the prodigal son. We have not come back of our own accord; our Father has taken the initiative to go out searching for us to bring us back. Furthermore it is not simply that we are destitute; rather, far more grievous, our sins have sold us into slavery to Satan. We are like

Dr. Faust; we have, by rejecting the authority of God in our lives, sold our souls to the devil himself, which is why Faust's story, if we understand it, sends chills up our spine. For Jesus Christ had to enter the domain of Satan to redeem our souls. He had to walk through the black, yawning chasm of hell, past the leering faces of those who had claimed our souls in order to buy us back at the cost of His lifeblood. *But that is how much He loved us!* In his letter to the Galatians, Paul reminds us that we were slaves to the powers of darkness: "But when the time had fully come, God sent his Son, born of a woman, born under law, to redeem those under law"—and those who faced the penalty of the law—"that we might receive the full rights of sons. Because you are sons, God sent the Spirit of his Son into our hearts, the Spirit who calls out, '*Abba,* Father.' So you are no longer a slave, but a son; and since you are a son, God has made you also an heir" (Galatians 4:4–7).

In the Roman culture into which the gospel first came, adoption was different from our practice. It involved not infants, but grown adults who were adopted by wealthy and childless patrons for the specific purpose of establishing a legal heir to an estate. The one doing the adopting, of course, chose a person who had proved himself responsible, a man of integrity and self-discipline who would uphold the family name and make wise use of the resources he inherited. But one of the astonishing things about God's adoption of us is that He has done it precisely when we had nothing to offer. And this is where the Spirit comes in to shape us to be the son or daughter our heavenly Father might be proud to adopt. Romans 8 is all about the work of the Holy Spirit.

The first thing the Holy Spirit does in this adoption, according to Romans 8:16, is assure us of our place in God's family. Then He begins in us the work of transformation that will ultimately allow us to reflect the character of a true son or daughter.

The Spirit first makes us aware of the delightful fact that we may now call that distant and terrifying God *"Abba,"* Father. This has nothing to do with our moral achievement. We have not earned our place in His presence. It is simply an undeserved privilege. But it is the job of the Holy Spirit to show us that privilege.

We live in a world that is undergoing a huge and unsettling identity crisis. We don't know who we are or why our lives should have any value. We seek desperately to build our self-esteem, even while everything in our secular world says we are nothing but random beings on our way to no place in particular, cursed primarily with a self-awareness that desires something we can never achieve. But God says, "No, that's not it at all. Listen to Me! You *really are* somebody, not because you happen to be more intelligent than any other beast, but because you are not a beast at all! You have been made in My image. You can know and enjoy My glory and share in the delight of all My privileges. What makes you doubt this is the knowledge deep within you, stirred by the conscience I have given you, that you have rejected the good that I offered and ruined the experiment I began in you. But I have good news. I have redeemed you. I have paid the price for you. You are Mine. And if you will accept it by faith, I will restore you to the place I have reserved for you in My family. Not only that, but I will transform you by My Spirit into the person I created you to be." Now there is reason for self-esteem! God loves us, and His Spirit is at work in the hearts of His children to restore us to His own image.

TRANSFORMATION INTO FAMILY LIKENESS: SANCTIFICATION

This involves a process that we will consider in the next chapter. Theologians have called it "sanctification." But first we need to know that when we are received into God's family by adoption, we receive His Spirit, and that Spirit begins to transform us into His image. "Dear friends," John informs us, "now we are children of God, and what we will be has not yet been made known." You can hear a wonderful sense of anticipation here in John's words. He continues, "But we know that when he appears, we shall be like him, for we shall see him as he is" (1 John 3:2). You and I, if we belong to Christ, are one day going to be incredibly special! We have the potential right now, and if we have been united with Him, He is in the process of shaping us to be like Himself.

Do you know where we got the phrase "spit 'n' image"? We say things like, "He's the spit 'n' image of his father." Perhaps you will be surprised to know it has nothing to do with spitting. The truth is this is a mispronunciation of an English dialect that was intended to say "the spirit and image." You and I really are intended to be the "spit 'n' image" of Jesus Christ. God the Father, when He adopts us into His family, places His Spirit in us to form us in His image. We see this perfectly displayed in Jesus Christ, the model of the person God intends for us to be. The whole of the eighth chapter of Romans goes into some detail to show us how, through the power of that Spirit working within us, we are to put to death the distorted habits of our natural bodies so that we might come more and more to resemble His Son.

PRIVILEGES OF ADOPTION: GOD'S FREE GIFTS

If you have surrendered your heart to Jesus Christ, God has adopted you into His family. That's already done. But I wonder if you have stopped to think about the enormous privileges that are yours as a result. The Westminster Confession (XII.I) calls our attention to most of these. As His children, we now have His name legitimately put upon us. A good name bears with it a reputation and a respect that gives us access to people and places and opportunities we could never have approached on our own. "You mean you're the president's daughter!" Or, "Wow! You're related to C. S. Lewis? Come with me; I want to introduce you to some of my friends!" Think what it means to be related to someone special, to have that person's name. Think what it means for us to bear the name of Jesus Christ!

Another great privilege of our place within God's family is our open access to the Father. The sovereign Lord is never too busy or distracted to turn His attention to us and to listen to whatever we have to say. What a privilege it is for us to be invited to pray! Do you neglect that privilege? Suppose you had such access to the president of the United States, or the chief justice of the Supreme Court, or even the mayor of your city. Would you despise the privilege of having the person's ear privately? What an amazing thing to be able to talk at any time to a God who wants to hear what is on our hearts and who wants to include our concerns in His governance of the world!

As adopted children, John reminds us in his first epistle, we also have the liberty of fellowship with the Father and with His Son, Jesus Christ. I can remember some very lonely days when I first arrived at college, away from my own home for the first time, knowing no one and having no access to any place where I felt I belonged. Sometimes I walked the streets in the evening and saw families gathered around their tables in the warm light of their homes conversing animatedly, and I would feel so excluded and alone the pain was almost palpable. But in the doctrine of adoption is the image of our Lord, rushing out into the street to embrace us and say, "Come in! Come in! We have been waiting for you. There is a place at the hearth with your name on it. Join us. Don't even think about passing by!" With adoption into God's family comes fellowship with Him and with all who share the favor of His household.

And this place in His family is a position secured by His commitment to us. The young woman in our opening illustration learned that no matter how happy and hopeful she might become in a family's love, she could never count on it. But she wasn't looking for sympathy when she told her story. "I needed [that experience]," she said. "It brought me to God." You see, she had found in Him the One she could always depend on. The love she had experienced before might have been withdrawn at any time if she did not please her new parents or if they tired of her presence. But this does not happen with God. He is absolutely faithful. He never changes His mind. Having adopted us into His family, He pledges everything He has to maintain us in that position as His children, regardless of any failure or any flaw in us. You don't say to your kids when they fail, "That's it! You're out of here! You're not my son anymore. You're not my daughter." (You might be tempted at times, but you don't say it.) God is not even tempted to say that.

There is so much more. God offers us His counsel and His guidance. Romans 8:14 says the children of God are led by the Spirit of God—that internal guidance He gives us through His Spirit. We are not lost. We are not left without direction. We have His all-knowing, wise, and loving counsel—not just a set of rules to restrict our options, but principles and ideals by which to set our course through life in a way that will bring us the most fulfillment and joy.

Along with this guidance comes our heavenly Father's encouragement and discipline. In baptismal vows, parents are urged to bring up their children in the "nurture and admonition" of the Lord. This is the positive and the negative side of parenting. The best parents both warn their children away from destructive behavior and encourage them toward productive and rewarding behavior. God does the same with us if we are His children. He does not punish us, but He will certainly discipline us. The difference is that punishment looks backward to past failure, but He has already dealt with that by accepting the punishment for us. Discipline looks forward to a future in which we are learning to do it better, and it is a token of God's love for us that His discipline shapes us in that way.

Of course we gain as well the promise of His fatherly protection and care. In the Sermon on the Mount, Matthew 6:25–34, Jesus stated it clearly. He said in essence, "What are you worrying about anyway? Why are you worrying about what you're going to eat or what you're going to drink or where you are going to sleep or what you are going to wear? Do you think I can't take care of My own children? Your heavenly Father knows that you need such things." He concludes, "But seek first his kingdom and his righteousness, and all these things will be given to you as well."

Here, I believe, is the practical truth that may govern everything we have learned about adoption. All these things and more are ours as God's children. Indeed, ultimately He has made us heirs to His entire fortune. "Heirs of God and co-heirs with Christ," Paul says in Romans 8:17. The difference between an heir and a co-heir is that an heir receives some particular percentage of an estate, and a co-heir along with others inherits the entire estate! You and I are destined to share the entire estate with our brother Jesus Christ, the only begotten Son of God!

But as you reflect on these truths, you may say, "That sounds delightful, but I don't feel it in my heart. I don't experience this measure of love." If you don't feel like your faith has introduced you to such wealth, if you don't experience the privilege of bearing Christ's name; if you don't have any sense that God is listening to your prayers; if you can't conjure up the experience of intimate communion with the Lord (the sort lost in the Garden of Eden); if you have not been enjoying any of the privileges we have named here and you continue to worry about God's forgiveness, acceptance, care, and protection—you don't have to go looking for some special blessing of God's Spirit that will miraculously "give you the feeling." God never asks us to do that.

On the contrary, Jesus has given us the clue here in

Matthew 6 for getting *beyond* our feelings. He says in effect, "You're worrying too much about your feelings; it's a waste of time. Rather what you have forgotten is the first priority." Our first job, our primary responsibility and privilege, is to seek God Himself, to seek His face, to prize His fellowship, to contemplate His person and character, to focus our attention on who He is. And as we do that, His Spirit will go to work within us to accomplish all the rest. He has chosen us and made us His own, and He is the One who will accomplish what He has set out to do because we are His children, and He loves us!

NOTE

1. Keith Miller, *Habitation of Dragons* (Waco, Tex.: Word, 1970), 183–84.
2. Ibid.

Chapter Eight

RESTORING

GOD'S IMAGE

Of Sanctification

Westminster Confession, chap. XIII;
Romans 6:1–14

*N*ick stood in front of the bathroom sink looking dully at his image reflecting back from the mirror. The low, artificial light cast his shadow on the wall. It was after midnight and the house was asleep. But Nick could not shake the deep sense of dissatisfaction with his life that had plagued him all through the day. It had been his fortieth birthday, and everybody came to celebrate, joke about his "advanced age," and tell stories about him.

It wasn't that he really felt old, however. It was just that it didn't seem his life was adding up to be what he had always thought and hoped it would be. He was doing quite well at his job, his marriage was OK, and he loved his kids even though they sometimes disappointed him—but he really didn't like the person he saw in the mirror very much. He had always thought he would turn out to be a better person.

Nick had been a Christian most of his life. He really want-

ed to please God, but for the last ten or fifteen years it seemed like he wasn't making any progress in his Christian walk. It wasn't that he was an especially bad person; most people thought very highly of him. But all sorts of sins continued to plague him no matter how seriously he wanted to be rid of them—anger and lust and pride and laziness—and now and then when he stopped to look at himself he found it very discouraging. Sins he had confessed a thousand times kept coming back to haunt him, and the person he saw in the mirror didn't look very Christlike at all. Why wasn't he getting any better? Was there any real hope that he might yet become the person he truly wanted to be?

Nick's concern has been felt by every true Christian. Coming to Christ is a powerful, revitalizing experience. To know that we are loved by God and we have been forgiven for all our sins and accepted into His family is the most incredible discovery anyone could ever make. The freedom justification brings from that gnawing sense of guilt is indescribable. But sooner or later we begin to want more than forgiveness—much more than forgiveness. We want to be freed from the debilitating power of sin in our lives.

Sometimes when we are very young, it's just great to know we are forgiven. We think, *Now that's a deal; I can go on sinning and I don't have to worry about anything. I'll always be forgiven.* But as we walk with the Lord for a time we start to think, *I don't want to do that. I don't want to spend my life sinning. How can I get out from under the power of sin in my life? How can I begin to grow and in some small way at least come to resemble Jesus Christ?* The troubling reality is what the apostle Paul confessed in that anguished and powerful seventh chapter of Romans:

When I want to do good, evil is right there with me. For in my inner being I delight in God's law; but I see another law at work in the members of my body, waging war against the law of my mind and making me a prisoner of the law of sin at work within my members. What a wretched man I am! Who will rescue me from this body of death? (Romans 7:21–24)

The problem is that our sin has not only rendered us guilty, but it has shattered the image of God in us, as we learned in chapter 3. As a result, it was not enough for God to declare us "not guilty" when Jesus Christ paid the penalty for our sins. Something has to happen to effect a real change in our lives—to restore God's image in us. And what God has devised in His wisdom and compassion is what theologians have called the process of sanctification.

Most of us don't use the word "sanctification" very much, but it is a simple and powerful word. To sanctify something is to make it holy. If it is a person, sanctification means to shape him so he resembles God Himself. And this is what every true Christian longs for desperately. A lot of people, for one reason or another, want to be around the church community. They may simply long to be accepted by somebody. They may want to appropriate the church's power or to take advantage of its resources. Church growth experts encourage us to provide a smorgasbord of activities and services, religious or otherwise, in which people may take part. But a true believer longs for holiness. A true believer desires to become like Jesus Christ. Is that the desire of your heart?

THE GOAL OF SANCTIFICATION

This desire for holiness leads us to the goal of sanctification. The goal of sanctification is to restore the image of God in us. The Westminster Confession points out that there are at least three things happening to contribute to the goal of sanctification. The first is that *sin's mastery or dominion over us is destroyed* (XIII.I). "Don't you know," Paul said in Romans 6, "that all of us who were baptized into Christ Jesus were baptized into his death? . . . Our old self was crucified with him so that the body of sin might be done away with, that we should no longer be slaves to sin—because anyone who has died has been freed from sin" (vv. 3, 6).

This means that we don't *have* to sin anymore. At one time sin was our master and we were its slave, but that is no longer true. In the past, sin could make us do its will, and we were powerless against it, but now we have a new master. Sin's slavehold on us has been broken. A new force is at work in us now, a force far more powerful than the force of sin. It is exceedingly comforting to know that Christ's death on the cross has set us free from our bondage to sin. It is as if we had been held for ransom, bound and gagged in some dismal prison. But Jesus Christ paid that ransom and set us free. Sanctification means first of all that we can begin to breathe the fresh air of freedom. We do not have to serve sin any longer. We are no longer sin's slaves. We have been united with Christ in His death and His resurrection.

Unfortunately, however, that is not our *experience.* Part of the reason is that we have been slaves to sin for so long that debilitating habits have formed in our lives.

Our bodies, our minds, and our spirits move quite naturally and spontaneously along the grooves carved out by sinful thoughts and sinful patterns of behavior. Getting out of these ruts is not easy, as anyone who has tried knows. So we have to go a step further. Sin's mastery over us has been destroyed, but the second thing contributing to the goal of sanctification is *a slow weakening of these tenacious and destructive habits,* coupled with the positive side, the third activity, which is *a slow and steady strengthening of the new nature that God's Spirit has formed within us.* Those are the three things the Westminster Confession says are a part of sanctification.

Sin's dominion over us is destroyed, tenacious habits are slowly but progressively weakened, and the new nature that God has placed within us through His Spirit is gradually nurtured and strengthened. Again Paul says in Romans 6:19, "I put this in human terms because you are weak in your natural selves. Just as you used to offer the parts of your body in slavery to impurity and to ever-increasing wickedness, so now offer them in slavery to righteousness leading to holiness."

The ultimate goal of sanctification is holiness. Throughout the Bible God challenges us to be holy because He is holy. We were created to reflect His glory. Holiness is what we are all about. So God desires to eliminate sin from our lives and ultimately to conform us completely to the image of His Son. What He has begun in us, He promises in Philippians 1:6, He will accomplish. However, it is very important to recognize that this is a lifelong process that will not be complete until we are with the Lord. We should never say "sanctification" without saying "the process of sanctification." We should

127

never think that in some magical way we may suddenly be transformed overnight. It doesn't happen. Sanctification is a process.

Throughout the church's history, some have taught that we can achieve perfection in this lifetime. It is true that sin is dethroned in a moment with the death and resurrection of Jesus Christ. But what the Bible calls the mortification of sinful habits, rooting them out and building new habits, is a long and sometimes arduous process. Eugene Peterson has written a book on discipleship in an instant society called *A Long Obedience in the Same Direction*. The title alone is an appropriate and encouraging word to all serious Christians. Sanctification simply doesn't happen in an instant. It happens as a result of a "long obedience in the same direction." The old lusts, our Confession says, are "more and more weakened," while we are "more and more quickened and strengthened in all saving graces, to the practice of true holiness."

THE SERIOUSNESS OF DISCIPLESHIP

It is impossible for me to stress too much the gravity of this process in our lives. Our world doesn't think much about holiness, but we had better be thinking about it. This is not an optional "upper division" course in discipleship for elite Christians. This is for all of us. The problem is, we are engaged in a tremendous spiritual battle. Satan is contending for our very souls, and he is doing a very good job of it while we're not paying attention! The Westminster Confession calls it "a continual and irreconcilable war" (XIII.II). The Confession warns that some remnants of corruption continue to cling to our bodies and our spirits throughout our lives. It is important to understand that. We are fallen, and we will struggle with this as long as we live. Nevertheless it is a battle we must enter with all the resources available to us, for "without holiness," God's Word declares, "no one will see the Lord" (Hebrews 12:14b).

I hope you take the issue of sin in your life very seriously. Each of us needs to be challenged to *wake up* to the battle being waged for our souls—waged most dangerously when we are paying the least attention. Every sin we commit is a contradiction of God's holiness, a contradiction of the very reason for which we were created. Every sin we commit, therefore, deserves God's wrath. Furthermore, in a very practical way, every sin we commit deepens the rut in which we find ourselves and strengthens the hold of sin over our lives. Reflecting on this truth some time ago, I wrote in my journal from painful experience, "No sin, no matter how seemingly innocuous, can be left untended in your life, for it is the nature of sin to grow and to claim an increasing portion of your soul. Often, when the threat finally becomes evident, sin's foothold has grown so strong that displacing it becomes all but impossible."

All but impossible. Not impossible, and I want to stress that as well. Whatever our experience and whatever our failure to date, we may have made it more difficult for ourselves, but it is not impossible. The dominion of sin in our lives has been broken by the death and resurrection of Jesus Christ.

The power of God's Spirit is at work in you, and it is not impossible even today—no matter how long you have practiced that sin—it is not impossible to begin to root it out. That's what God means when He says the dominion of sin has been destroyed. It's possible to do better. No matter how discouraged you may become, it is very important for you never to give up in that battle. Satan wants you to give up. He wants you to say, "I've been working at this for years; I've made no progress; it's time to give it up!" Absolutely not! It is a process. It is a day-by-day dependence upon God. Don't give up. "[My] mercies," God says, "are new every morning" (Lamentations 3:23 KJV). When you get up every morning it's a fresh day, and you can start all over again and walk with the Lord. The promise of sanctification is that God *will* accomplish His purpose in us. "He who began a good work in you, will carry it on to completion until the day of Christ Jesus" (Philippians 1:6).

THE AGENT OF SANCTIFICATION

And this brings us to the agent of sanctification. If the goal of sanctification is our holiness, the agent of sanctification is God's Spirit. It is God's Spirit alone who makes us holy. It is not our great personal discipline. It is not our remarkable skills. It is not our carefully guarded piety. It is God's Spirit alone. You and I must understand that this goal of holiness will never be achieved as the result of our supreme efforts. It is something God alone can accomplish in us.

OUR DEPENDENCE ON THE HOLY SPIRIT

One of our greatest weaknesses is our failure to recognize our absolute dependence upon God's Spirit. We are very self-confident. We think we can do nearly anything if we are willing to make an effort. We say, "I can do that, I can do that." But you cannot please God. You cannot be holy by your own efforts. It is impossible. Only God's Spirit at work within you can make that happen. It is not that God doesn't enlist our efforts toward this goal of holiness, because He does. But our efforts would never be enough to achieve it. If we rely on our own resolution, if we rely on our own strength of purpose, if we rely on our own self-discipline, we are going to fail. You and I must, above all, be aware of our own weakness. That is where holiness begins. When we recognize our weakness and our dependence upon God, confess our sins, and ask Him day by day, moment by moment, for His support and His help, we are on our way to sanctification.

Focusing on our weaknesses, of course, flies in the face of the prevailing philosophy of our day. Our society, which has humanity as its absolute center, can't afford to say that. Our society says we must emphasize our strengths and ignore, as much as possible, our weaknesses. God's Word says if you don't know you are weak, you will never be strong. Knowledge of our weaknesses moves us to dependence upon God, who is the only true source of our strength. "My power," God says, "is made perfect in weakness" (2 Corinthians 12:9). I think that is a tremendously encouraging word. You are looking at how many times and ways you have failed, but God says His strength is made perfect in you, particularly in your weaknesses and in your failure. When the apostle Paul, a Pharisee who had always boasted in his strengths, finally recognized that, he concluded instead: "Therefore I will boast all the more gladly about my weaknesses, so that Christ's power may rest on me" (2 Corinthians 12:9). He had grasped the heart of the challenge. So he said with a properly placed confidence, "For when I am weak, then I am strong" (v. 10b). That is where it begins for all of us who are Christians.

SCRIPTURAL PROGRESSION REGARDING SANCTIFICATION

A fascinating progression from the Old to the New Testament is very instructive concerning this process of sanctification. The whole Old Testament is about the Law of God. It tells us what sort of people we ought to be. The Old Testament describes the holiness God requires. The problem is, as is quite evident in the whole history of the Old Testament, we cannot do it. We know what we ought to do, but we can't do it. That is the problem with every one of the world's great religions. Each will give its list, its Five Pillars or its Eight-Fold Path, like our Ten Commandments, which say what a person ought to do. But the problem has always been that we cannot do it. We know how we should act, but we find ourselves incapable of living up even to our own standards.

So the prophets in the Old Testament began to predict something exciting. They predicted that God was going to do something very different. The time is coming when God will take an entirely new approach to our continuing failure, Jeremiah said with a compelling sense of anticipation.

> "The time is coming," declares the Lord, "when I will make a new covenant with [my people]. It will not be like the covenant I made with their forefathers . . . because they broke [that] covenant. . . . This is the covenant I will make. . . . I will put my law in their minds and write it on their hearts." (31:31–33)

God said through Ezekiel, "I will give you a new heart and put a new spirit in you ... and move you to follow my decrees and be careful to keep my laws" (36:26–27).

You see, knowing what we ought to do was not enough. God needed to motivate us from the inside to do what was right. To do that He knew He must change our hearts. And that, of course, is what began to happen on the Day of Pentecost. This process of sanctification, a wholly new thing in God's economy, began. God poured out His Spirit on all believers to equip them to obey from the heart. The apostle Paul says:

> Those who live according to the sinful nature have their minds set on what that nature desires; but those who live in accordance with the Spirit have their minds set on what the Spirit desires. The mind of sinful man is death, but the mind controlled by the Spirit is life and peace. . . . You, however, are controlled not by the sinful nature but by the Spirit, if the Spirit of God lives in you. (Romans 8:5–9)

So there is our hope. The agent of change is the Holy Spirit of God, and He has placed that Spirit in every believer. It is that Spirit alone, working in us, who can make any substantial changes.

THE MEANS OF SANCTIFICATION

Now that is all well and good. We understand it, perhaps, in theory. But how does it actually happen? How does real change take place? What are the means of sanctification? The goal of sanctification is to make us holy; the agent of sanctification is the Holy Spirit at work from the inside. But what do you and I have to do in a practical way? How can we make this happen? Nick, the man in our opening illustration, had been a Christian for a long time, but his life was not being transformed. Where was God's Spirit? Why wasn't He changing him? What was the problem?

What is *our* problem? We have been inclined to think the problem is that we have to try harder. We have simply not given enough effort. But the message of God's Word is that our efforts can never achieve the holiness God requires. Some people have concluded, "Well, if our efforts won't achieve it, then we will just have to be passive.'Let go and let God' do it through us." But you know that is not what the Bible says. It never says, "Stop trying and let God work through you."

This *sounds* very spiritual, but how would you actually do it? What, specifically, would you do? What if you made a conscious attempt to sit back and pray and just let Him change you, but nothing happened? Obviously there is still something missing from our formula. If anything changes in our lives, it will indeed be the Holy Spirit who accomplishes it, but what are the means of this sanctification? Is there anything we can do to make this happen? There is a great clue in Philippians 4:13. Notice that it does *not* say here that God will do everything through me. Rather it says, "I can do everything *through him* who gives me strength." I don't do it by my own strength. But neither does He expect me to be passive while He does it through me. The crucial formula is, *I* do it *through Him!* This is an all-important distinction.

Sanctification is the process through which you and I are shaped into God's image. It involves *our* actions made effective through the power of *His* Spirit. That is why Paul said earlier in his letter to the Philippians, "Continue to work out your salvation with fear and trembling, for it is God who works in you to will and to act according to his good purpose" (Philippians 2:12–13). You see, we are saved by grace, but we have a job to do—to work out what God is working within us.

Sanctification involves our conscious and deliberate acts of obedience, acts of which we are capable only through the power of His Spirit. This winning combination can take place *only* if we recognize our weakness, consciously and continually call upon Him for His support, and rely upon Him for His power. In Romans 6:11–13 we are told, "Count [or consider] yourselves dead to sin," and (a very practical thing), "offer the parts of your body to him as instruments of righteousness." What are the parts of our bodies? This is as practical as it gets. The parts of our bodies are clearly our hands, our feet, our mouths, our eyes, our minds, and so forth. We are to "offer [these] parts of your body to him as instruments of righteousness."

GOD AND US: THE COOPERATIVE EFFORT

Let me illustrate this cooperative effort between ourselves and God's Spirit. Suppose an amateur mountain climber, carried away by the exhilarating beauty of his surroundings and perhaps deceived by unusually fine conditions, overreaches his ability. Eventually he finds himself brought back to reality, precariously perched high on the face of a sheer mountain where he has fallen onto an inaccessible ledge. He does not have the skills or the equipment to get down, so a deep terror begins to arise in his heart as the night closes in and the weather begins to change. He realizes that if nothing intervenes, he will die on the face of that mountain. He can put forth his best effort, but thousands of feet up on this sheer granite wall in the darkness, he will eventually and certainly fall to his death.

As the inevitability of his fate dawns upon him, as he shakes almost uncontrollably in the cold and the darkness, he hears another climber, this one equipped with all the essential climbing gear and carrying emergency supplies, working his way toward him along the face of the rock. As he approaches, the newcomer observes, "You seem to be in serious trouble!" And then, as he swings over beside the tiny ledge to which our imperiled climber is clinging desperately, he says, "I would be glad to help you down if you will trust me."

Given his awareness of his predicament, I doubt if our friend would respond, "No, thank you, I want to do this myself." On the other hand he might be forgiven for thinking, *I don't know how you can do that. It's dark and cold and wet, and I have no real mountain-climbing skills. You can't carry me down off the face of this mountain, and I can't make it down on my own. I don't see any way out of this mess. It's hopeless!*

"Don't worry," the second climber says. "I can get you down, but you'll have to cooperate with me. Here, let me put this jacket on you, and slip this harness around you, and tie you on the rope with me, first of all, so you will be secure. Now, listen carefully. I'm going to give you detailed instructions and you'll have to do exactly as I say. First I want you to jam your hand into this crack in the rock, and I will guide your foot down to a little toehold just out of sight below you. Trust me. Slip your foot over the ledge. Let's go." And so, inch by inch, step by step, the rescuer brings our friend down the mountain, off that sheer rock face to safety, enabling him to do something he was entirely incapable of doing on his own.

Do you see how it works? There are several important things for us to recognize about this illustration. First, the victim had to acknowledge his own helplessness before he could be helped. As long as he was confident he could do this on his own, things were hopeless for him. He had to recognize that his own efforts were not going to be adequate to save his life. Second, he had to come to depend utterly upon the one who offered him help. He had to trust his life into his hands, and he had to be willing to do anything he said. But finally, he had to put forth a very significant effort on his own.

It is exactly the same with us in our relationship to Jesus Christ. He will not help us until we are willing to acknowledge our own helplessness. This is where it all begins. We must realize that our own best efforts will never be adequate to make us holy. Next, we must cast ourselves utterly upon His care with a willingness to believe Him and cooperate with Him in every way. Obviously, in the end this will not be a passive thing. It will require a significant effort on our part that He alone can transform into genuine holiness. That is the means of sanctification.

The whole of sanctification, then, depends upon our abiding in Jesus Christ, walking with Him, listening to Him, obeying Him, asking for His help, depending upon Him moment by moment, day by day. God's Spirit at work in us stirs our desire for this intimate communion with Jesus Christ. But you and I have a job to do. We need to concentrate our thoughts, our interest, and our efforts upon the cultivation of that union with Jesus Christ, that relationship, that constant communion with Him. Our hearts, our minds, our wills must be set upon Jesus Christ and upon His holiness if we are to become the persons He created us to be. But what a thrill to find ourselves progressing toward that goal! Out of that precarious place where we were certain to lose our lives, we suddenly find ourselves capable of things we had not even imagined before, because God's Spirit is at work within us.

I want to encourage you in this walk of sanctification that you will be involved in until the day Christ calls you home. The dominion of sin over your life has been broken by Jesus' death and resurrection. You are not going to fall to your death. You may slip or stumble from time to time, but you are "on the rope" with Jesus Christ if you have committed your life to Him, and He will not let you fall so far that you cannot recover. On the other hand, each fall leaves you with abrasions that are painful and that may have difficulty healing. Indeed, some may handicap you for the rest of your life. Cooperating with Christ in this adventure is your first and best priority. Concentrate every effort upon learning Christlikeness from Him, seeing how He walks and walking also in that way. That is how God sets about the process of restoring His image in us. By this and this alone is our salvation worked out, and this alone is our joy!

Chapter Nine

BEYOND

OURSELVES

Of Faith & Works

Westminster Confession, chaps. XIV–XVI;
Ephesians 2:1–10

A cluster of aspen, Black Hills spruce, and ponderosa pine hides our little cabin in one corner of our nation's outback. High above the cabin stands an impressive outcropping of Pre-Cambrian granite that is unnamed in the official annals of The National Forest Service, but that has been known to our family for three generations as "Steamboat." It is a three-tiered, razorlike ridge, little more than six feet wide at the top. Stony walls fall away in a dizzying, near-vertical drop of several hundred feet, but the ridge is enticing because it commands a stunning, 360-degree vista of nearly the entire range of the Black Hills. It has become a highly anticipated climbing destination for our family each summer—something of an annual pilgrimage —a touchstone by which to measure our growth and reestablish our place within the land.

From the time that each of our children had to be carried in a backpack, we have brought them with us to the top, partly to let them share the exhilaration of the magnificent view, and partly to let them enjoy the tremendous sense of accomplishment that goes with the successful achievement of any difficult goal. Of course there are genuine risks involved, and when the children are small, whether they realize it or not, it is really their parents who get them to the top and ensure that they do not fall to their death.

One recent summer we took our children and several of their cousins with us, including our four-year-old niece who was quite confident that she needed no help. "Don't worry," she said to me as she scrambled along the ridge just inches from a sheer drop to certain death, trying to wrestle her hand free from my iron grip, "I can do it."

"I do worry," I said, knowing she would not understand, "and I'm not going to let go of your hand."

It was, I thought, as I stood there on that mountain with her life literally in my hands, a vivid demonstration of our blithe ignorance concerning our utter dependence upon God. "Don't worry," we say to Him as we teeter on the brink of eternal destruction, "I can do it." But without His gracious protection and care, our doom would be absolutely certain. We can't draw a breath without Him! *We cannot traverse the precarious escarpments and precipices of death and hell in our own strength. . . . But even as we consider that, even as we raise the question of whether there may be some limitation to our judgment and ability, our wounded pride, like that of my four-year-old niece, begins to object. We resist any suggestion of weakness or helplessness on our part, and we begin to plot ways of slipping free of God's grasp in order to prove ourselves.*

One of the most terrifying insights I have ever

gained from my study of the Scriptures is that, in the end, all of us receive the desire of our hearts. If we set our hearts on seeking God, He promises to pardon and to embrace us eternally. But if the unrelenting desire of our hearts is to be free of His grip, there actually does come a day when He will release us to our own chosen fate.

STEP ONE: REPENTANCE

It is for this reason that the first and absolutely essential step in our experience of salvation is repentance. In the Bible, repentance involves not simply a remorse for our sins or failures (or for being found out for our sins and failures); repentance involves a turning away from our sin. The Westminster Confession identifies it as the prerequisite of life (chapter XV). We will never know real life until we first turn away from the behavior that leads only to death.

You see, each of us clings to certain things we hope will lead to life and happiness and peace. This may be material things, it may be success, it may be particular relationships; but fundamentally we cling to the myth of our own adequacy. Our pride is such that we do not want to admit any limitations or weaknesses that we cannot overcome: "Don't worry. I can do it." But in clinging to the myth of our own all-sufficiency, we ensure our eventual downfall. To repent is to let go of this lie of our own sufficiency. We are not capable of pleasing a holy God, and we are not clever enough to avoid death.

If I may paraphrase the Westminster Confession on repentance, the ability to repent is a gift of God's grace, and by this gift of grace a sinner is enabled to see not only the danger, but the ugliness and distortion of sin. Actually the Westminster Confession chooses an even less palatable description. It speaks of the "filthiness and odiousness of [our] sins" (XV.II). Further, repentance sees the ugliness of sin in relationship to the beauty and wholeness (or holiness) of God; and, in seeing that, it is moved to turn away from sin and commit to walk in the way of God's commandments. That is a fine definition of repentance: to turn away from the ugliness and destructiveness of sin, toward the God who offers us life. For my niece on the mountain it would be a matter of recognizing the foolishness of her belief in her self-sufficiency, ceasing her struggle to pursue her own path, and accepting the proffered assistance.

Ephesians 2:1–3 says that when we insisted on following the ways of this world, "gratifying the cravings of our sinful nature and following its desires and thoughts," we were bound for death. It is absolutely essential, therefore, that we first let go of those things that lead to death. That is fundamental to repentance. We need to be clear about this. The Confession reminds us that repentance does not satisfy our guilt before a holy God. It doesn't earn our pardon. God must deal with that; indeed, He *has* dealt with that and may therefore offer it to us freely. Yet repentance is indispensable for our salvation. And the reason is, we cannot know life until we have released our grip on death.

STEP TWO: FAITH

But a second step is equally as essential as repentance, and that is faith. If repentance is letting go of what cannot possibly hold us, then faith is clinging to what can certainly hold us.

Admittedly, the concept of faith is an elusive one. Sometimes we use the word to express little more than our opinion of something. "I'm not certain, but I *believe* this to be true." That may mean that we *hope* it is true, or that, at least at the present moment, it seems more likely to be true than the alternatives. By "faith" we may mean little more than an intellectual assent with few, if any, implications for our daily lives. Or we may use the word to describe a "leap of faith," a commitment to act with no very clear certainty of the outcome. Such "faith," I think, speaks more of our own inner condition than it does of anything outside ourselves.

True faith, by contrast, involves both our inner convictions *and* the object of our faith. Faith is indeed a commitment, but it must always be a commitment *to* something. And obviously the trustworthiness of the object to which we commit ourselves in faith is of paramount importance. The well-known Scottish theologian John Murray pointed out that there are three elements in faith. The first is *knowledge.* Sometimes we think of faith and knowledge as opposites: either we *know* something to be true, or in the absence of knowledge we just *have faith* that it is true. It would be enormously risky, however, and potentially disastrous for us to place our faith in something indiscriminately without any knowledge of its worthiness. True faith does not begin in a vacuum. It begins with knowledge; it begins with facts that we can glean from observation and analysis.

But knowledge alone, even knowledge of which we are entirely convinced, is not faith. The second element of faith is *conviction,* or more precisely, personal conviction. Faith recognizes the personal relevance of knowledge. It is not only being aware of the truth, but being convinced in my heart of the significance of that truth for my own life. I may know intellectually that certain drugs will kill me, but such knowledge is worthless if I am not personally convinced that I must avoid those drugs if I am to survive.

But even this, of course, is not enough. Not only must my mind and my heart or emotions be convinced, but I must be willing to act on that knowledge and on that conviction. The third, then, and most important aspect of faith is the action of our *will*—not just our mind and our heart, but our will. We know and believe, but we must ultimately be willing to place our *trust* in that which is the object of our faith. It does us no good simply to *believe* something; we must *act* on our belief. Faith is never complete until we have acted on our belief.

All of this—knowledge, conviction, and trust—constitutes our exercise of faith, but the other half of faith is equally indispensable. Our exercise of faith is meaningless if our trust is placed in an *object* that is not worthy of that trust. It works both ways. The object of our faith will be, of course, irrelevant if we do not act upon it. But likewise our act of faith is irrelevant if its object is not worthy of our trust. Both elements are absolutely vital to this exercise of faith. This is why we said earlier that repentance involves letting go of an unworthy object, and why we must say now that saving faith is clinging to an object that is entirely worthy of our trust.

Not long ago, my wife and I were backpacking along a wilderness area on the Washington coast with two friends. In many places sheer cliffs come right down to the water. At times hikers find themselves on a narrow strip of beach that is rapidly disappearing beneath the encroaching tides. The only option, other than allowing oneself to be crushed by the pounding surf, is to scale those rather formidable cliffs. Fortunately, where this is physically impossible, ladders consisting of wooden slats are attached to cables anchored in the rock—with a loose, hanging rope for a handrail. As we came to the first of these, which admittedly appeared quite daunting (especially in the falling rain), it quickly became evident that an act of faith was to be required of each of us. Of course the incoming surf, grasping at our heels, lent an urgency to our consideration!

For my part I did stop to examine and gain some knowledge about this ladder; and I determined in my head that it seemed securely constructed and would likely bear the weight of a climber, even with a fifty-pound pack on his back. Indeed, I was reasonably convinced that it would hold *me*. I came to truly *believe* that in my heart. Nevertheless for all my knowledge and belief, that ladder would do me no earthly good until I finally *trusted* myself to it by grasping it securely and beginning to climb, thereby allowing it to bear my weight and lift me above the surf. Faith is not complete until we make a *commitment*—until we *act upon* our knowledge and convictions.

It is precisely the same with the Christian faith. We must first of all have an adequate knowledge of the facts about Jesus Christ and about ourselves. From that knowledge we may become convinced that Jesus is our only way of salvation, that His death and resurrection are the only adequate means of our salvation. We may *believe* that Jesus is indeed the Son of God, and that He died for our sins, and that He rose again from the dead. But that knowledge and that conviction, no matter how heartfelt, will do us no good until we become willing to *act upon* that belief by *committing* ourselves to Him—casting ourselves upon His care, letting Him bear our weight, if you will.

Here is one of the most important things you will ever learn about faith: *We do not trust by believing; we trust by obeying.* When God says, "To do this will lead to death," the act of true faith is not to say, "I believe that with all my heart," but rather to avoid doing it! Likewise when God says, "To do this will lead to life," the act of true faith is not to *say,* "I believe that is true," but rather to *do* it! There is no faith without action, no trust without obedience!

| FAITH: A GIFT OF GOD'S GRACE

Lest we begin to boast about our great faith, however, the Westminster Confession points out that even this willingness to take God at His word and act upon His commands and promises does not really arise in us, but it "is the work of the Spirit of Christ in their hearts" (XIV.I). It is not something of which we can boast; it is itself a gift of God's grace. "For it is by grace you have been saved, through faith—and this not from yourselves, it is the gift of God—not by works, so that no one can boast," Paul explained in Ephesians 2:8–9.

God's Spirit, working in our hearts, convicts us of the truth of God's Word, the Confession explains. Furthermore that same Spirit enables us through the conviction of that Word, reinforced by worship and prayer, to actually change our conduct to bring it into conformity with

His will. This is what acting upon our faith is all about—a change in our conduct to bring us into conformity with the will of God. God's Spirit at work in us enables us to obey His commands, to fear His warnings, to embrace His promises, and ultimately to trust Jesus Christ alone for our salvation, as well as for life and the power for daily living.

All this puts our good works in perspective. In the first place, none of our own good works are good enough. They all fall short, as Paul points out in that well-known verse from Romans 3:23. As the Confession puts it, "As [our works] are good, they proceed from his Spirit; and as they are wrought by us, they are defiled, and mixed with so much weakness and imperfection, that they cannot endure the severity of God's judgment" (XVI.V). It is like my little niece whose very best efforts could only have ended in destruction, despite her encouragement for me not to worry. "All our righteous acts," Isaiah informs us, "are like filthy rags; we all shrivel up like a leaf, and like the wind our sins sweep us away" (64:6). Our very best efforts, the Confession explains, cannot bear the scrutiny of a holy God. As the gap between us and Him is infinite, we could never merit our salvation, and we could certainly never defeat death on our own. The cliff is too precipitous. We cannot scramble up on our own.

This does not mean, however, that there is no place for our efforts toward good works. Ephesians 2:10 reveals that we have been created for the very purpose of good works. To do good works is our ultimate goal. It is the destiny for which God has equipped us with His Spirit. Although it is true that only God is capable of truly good works, He nowhere suggests that we are relieved of our responsibility to do our very best. Indeed, this is the purpose for which we were created! It is just that we must begin with the acknowledgment that as humans, our best efforts will fall short, and it is only as His Spirit works within us that we may accomplish anything of value. "Therefore," Paul explains to his friends in Philippi, "as you have always obeyed . . . continue to work out your salvation with fear and trembling, for it is God who works in you to will and to act according to his good purpose" (2:12–13). Just do it, he says, because as you make the effort, God's Spirit is going to make it happen within you.

If I may go back to my niece once more to illustrate each of the three primary points in our consideration of faith and works, the first thing required of her was that she could let go of her cavalier belief that she can do this on her own. In her immaturity, of course, she was reluctant to do this. But at the very least she trusted my counsel enough to allow me to help. Second, and however reluctantly, she must continue to cling to my hand, or at least let me hold hers, for I was quite capable of bringing her to the mountaintop and securing her there if she would trust me. But third, following this formula, even under protest, she did in fact achieve the summit of that mountain and enjoy the spectacular view.

My niece found it difficult to understand, but a proper fear of the consequences of depending on her own abilities placed her in a position where she could accomplish things that far superseded her abilities! If she cooperated with me, her only limitation was *my* ability, not hers. It did require her effort. I didn't carry her to the top; she walked. Nevertheless it was through my support that she was enabled to reach the summit—something she could not have done on her own. Her faith, properly placed, could carry her far beyond her own limitations. And that is what God wants us to know about the limits of our own achievements and our glorious potential in Him.

You and I are offered the same promise in our Lord. Abandoning our conviction that we can do this on our own is what the first step, repentance, is all about. Otherwise we will continue resisting until God simply lets us have our way. The second step is our commitment in faith to trust Him by obeying Him. We would not be capable of this had He not placed His all-powerful Spirit within us. But filled with that Spirit, you and I can accomplish absolutely anything God wills for us. Our own limitations become utterly irrelevant. The only relevant issue is what He desires to accomplish in us.

In the early part of this century, Gladys Aylward, a missionary to China, was forced to flee for her life when the Japanese invaded Yangcheng. Unwilling to abandon the children with whom she worked, she attempted to lead more than a hundred orphans over the mountains toward free China. In their book *The Hidden Price of Greatness,* authors Ray Besson and Ranelda Mack Hunsicker tell about this heroic effort.

> During Gladys's harrowing journey out of war-torn Yangcheng, she grappled with despair as never before. After passing a sleepless night, she faced the morning with no hope of reaching safety. A 13-year-old girl in the group reminded her of their much-loved story of Moses and the Israelites crossing the Red Sea.

"But I am not Moses," Gladys cried in desperation.

"Of course you aren't," the girl said, "but Jehovah is still God!"

Gladys Aylward's limitations were utterly irrelevant. The only thing relevant was the person of the God who called her. Her task, like ours, was to cast herself upon His care by getting up each morning and obeying Him. That's all! The results were entirely in His hands, in the hands of the same God who led the Israelites across the Red Sea. The remarkable accomplishment of faith is that God will redeem your life from the pit and take you infinitely beyond your own limitations, accomplishing (as He wills) great things in you, if you will simply surrender yourself to Him in repentance and trust. The result is beautiful. The Westminster Confession says:

> These good works, done in obedience to God's commandments, are the fruits and evidences of a true and lively faith: and by them believers manifest their thankfulness, strengthen their assurance, edify their brethren, adorn the profession of the gospel, stop the mouths of the adversaries, and glorify God, whose workmanship they are, created in Christ Jesus thereunto, that, having their fruit unto holiness, they may have the end, eternal life. (XVI.II)

Nothing else will accomplish this. But this combination of repentance and faith can accomplish nothing less.

Chapter Ten

A WARNING

AND A PROMISE

Of the Perseverance of the Saints

Westminster Confession, chaps. XVII, XVIII;
Hebrews 3:6–4:13

*H*ey, Mom, don't worry about it! I still believe in God. Just because I don't go to church doesn't mean I'm not a Christian." But of course Randy's mother did worry about it. What does "being a Christian" mean, anyway? Shouldn't it make a difference in your life? Shouldn't you be able to tell if someone is truly a believer? She remembered how thrilled she had been when Randy came home from camp and announced that he had "asked Jesus into his heart." And things had been different in his life for quite a while after that. He began reading his Bible and going to the youth group regularly and listening to "Christian" music. He even thought for a while about going into the ministry.

But that had all begun to fade when he left for college. He started doing a lot of partying and drinking with his friends, eventually moved in with his girlfriend, and then stopped going *to church altogether. Whenever he talked to his mom he tried to reassure her, but she was not reassured.*

On the other hand, plenty of days she wondered about her own relationship with the Lord. Maybe her sins weren't as blatant as her son's, but they were pretty disappointing nonetheless. Just because she stayed active in her church didn't necessarily guarantee anything. How can anyone be certain whether he is really a Christian? How can anyone be absolutely certain where he stands with the living God?

The question is entirely legitimate, one we all need to consider. One of the central tenets of our faith is that salvation is strictly an act of God's grace. It is not something we earn through our own efforts. Since it is initiated and sustained by Him, as the Westminster Confession makes clear (XVII.I, II), we believe we cannot possibly lose our salvation. We don't believe that every day our salvation is on the line—that we may lose it today and regain it tomorrow and lose it again the next day. It depends upon Him, not us: "They, whom God hath accepted in his Beloved, effectually called, and sanctified by his Spirit, can neither totally nor finally fall away from the state of grace, but shall certainly persevere therein to the end, and be eternally saved" (XVII.I).

This is the truth the apostle Paul celebrated in Romans 8. After struggling with the reality of his own sin in that compelling seventh chapter, his eighth chapter fairly rings with delight in his knowledge that God has justified us in Christ Jesus, and therefore we no longer stand under His condemnation. Nothing at all (and he lists quite a few possibilities) can separate us from the love of God that is in Christ Jesus our Lord.

But if we start thinking this means we can do anything we please, we are suddenly brought up short by passages like Hebrews 6:4–6, where the author warns us,

> It is impossible for those who have once been enlightened, who have tasted the heavenly gift, who have shared in the Holy Spirit, who have tasted the goodness of the word of God and the powers of the coming age, if they fall away, to be brought back to repentance, because to their loss they are crucifying the Son of God all over again and subjecting him to public disgrace.

This is a frightening declaration! The writer goes on to explain by way of analogy,

> Land that drinks in the rain often falling on it and that produces a crop useful to those for whom it is farmed receives the blessing of God. But land that produces thorns and thistles is worthless and is in danger of being cursed. In the end it will be burned. (vv. 7–8)

You see, for all the experience we may have with the church and with God's Word, to determine the authenticity of such an experience it is legitimate to ask whether our lives give any indication that we have received new life from God's Spirit. The question is very straightforward: Is fruit being borne in our lives or not? If so, then there is blessing in store from God. If not, our destiny is destruction.

Jesus was certainly very direct about this. In His Sermon on the Mount He warned,

> By their fruit you will recognize them. Do people pick grapes from thornbushes, or figs from thistles? Likewise

every good tree bears good fruit, but a bad tree bears bad fruit. A good tree cannot bear bad fruit, and a bad tree cannot bear good fruit. Every tree that does not bear good fruit is cut down and thrown into the fire.

Then comes His explanation. He's not talking about trees; He's talking about you and me: "Not everyone who says to me, 'Lord, Lord,' will enter the kingdom of heaven, *but only he who does the will of my Father who is in heaven*" (Matthew 7:16–19, 21, italics added).

WHAT PERSEVERANCE DOES NOT MEAN

This is the solemn warning with which our study of the perseverance of the saints must begin. When the Bible talks about "perseverance," we need to be very certain we know what this does *not* mean. The perseverance of the saints does *not* mean that everyone who *professes* at some time in his life to have faith in Jesus Christ is guaranteed a place in heaven! That may come as a shock to those who have depended on some emotional experience from the past. But God's Word is clear. "Not everyone who says to me, 'Lord, Lord,' will enter the kingdom of heaven, *but only he who does the will of my Father who is in heaven*" (Matthew 7:21, italics added). Could it be more clear?

Perseverance does not mean salvation is guaranteed to everyone who has ever claimed to be a Christian, regardless of what they do after that. The Confession warns, "Hypocrites and other unregenerate men may vainly deceive themselves with false hopes and carnal presumptions of being in the favor of God." Such persons are then contrasted to those who "truly believe in

154

the Lord Jesus, and love him in sincerity, endeavoring to walk in all good conscience before him." Only the latter "may . . . be certainly assured that they are in the state of grace, and may rejoice in the hope of the glory of God" (XVIII.I). No one is assured of salvation whose life does not show the fruits of the grace he claims to have received.

It's like the riddle of the three frogs sitting on a log. Two of them *decided* to jump off. The question is, how many were left? You think the answer is one, but it's not. The answer is three. We're only told that they decided to jump off, not that they actually did it. Jesus says that just because you decide to call Him "Lord, Lord" doesn't mean you have a place in heaven. You have to do something about it! If He is truly your Lord, you will have to jump in and follow Him. Your belief has to make a difference in your life. Your words are meaningless if they are not followed up by actions. He isn't Lord because you *say* He is; He is Lord because you *do* what He says.

The Bible is very consistent about this. There is always a condition attached to the promise. *"If you hold to my teaching,"* Jesus says in John 8:31, "[then] you are really my disciples." Hebrews 3:14 says, "We have come to share in Christ *if we hold firmly till the end the confidence we had at first."* Or again, Jesus tells His followers in John 15:7–8, *"If you remain in me and my words remain in you, . . .* [then you show] yourselves to be my disciples." On the other hand, *"If anyone does not remain in me,* he is like a branch that is thrown away and withers; such branches are picked up, thrown into the fire and burned" (John 15:6).

Obviously it is presumptuous on our part to assume that we can say, "Lord, Lord," and do whatever we want. The perseverance of the saints does not mean that once we claim Jesus Christ as Lord, our actions are irrelevant and we can go ahead and sin with impunity. Quite the contrary, *our actions reveal whether or not we are actually in Christ*. The apostle John wrote about those who had once been active in the body of Christ, but who had turned away. He said, "They went out from us, but they did not really belong to us. For if they had belonged to us, they would have remained with us; but their going showed that none of them belonged to us" (1 John 2:19). That tells us something critically important about the perseverance of the saints. True saints will persevere. If they don't persevere, they are not true saints.

Hebrews 3 and 4 parallels this with the experience of the Israelites in the wilderness. Throughout the New Testament there is a close analogy between the Exodus and what we have come to know as salvation. Like a believer who is led out of bondage to sin, the Israelites were led out of slavery in Egypt. Indeed, Scripture likens their experience in crossing the Red Sea to baptism, which separated them from their former masters (1 Corinthians 10:2). Likewise our baptism marks the moment of our commitment to separate from the mastery of sin in our lives. The Israelites had to be nurtured and guided through the wilderness. We, too, need God's direction and nurture to survive the spiritual wilderness of our own day. God's intent was to lead them through that desert to find "rest" in the Promised Land, even as He intends to lead us through the desert of our culture today to the place He has prepared for us.

But God's solemn warning came by way of reference to that moment on the very border of the Promised Land when the Israelites, after receiving God's miraculous grace, chose to turn away from following Him in favor of their old life of slavery in Egypt. On that occasion God said, "Not one of the men who saw my glory and the miraculous signs I performed in Egypt and in the desert but who disobeyed me and tested me [these] ten times— not one of them will ever see the land I promised on oath to their forefathers. No one who has treated me with contempt will ever see it" (Numbers 14:22–23). This must of course be true for us spiritually as well. When we claim Jesus Christ as Lord, but then turn back from following Him and by our lives treat Him with contempt, we cannot expect Him to welcome us into His presence.

In Hebrews 3, the writer was extending a warning to individuals who had experienced God's grace, but who were in danger of falling away from following Him and thus forfeiting that blessing He had promised. He wrote, "See to it, brothers, that none of you has a sinful, unbelieving heart that turns away from the living God" (v. 12). We must understand how important this is. To turn away reveals that you never really trusted God in the first place. If you had trusted Him—truly trusted Him—you would have continued to follow Him. That's what trust is. So we prove our trust by continuing to follow Him.

Most readers will be familiar with Jesus' parable of the sower and the seed. It can be a very troubling parable. In that story He told of seed that fell on rocky ground and immediately sprang up; but since it had no roots, the sun scorched it and it eventually withered away. Jesus Himself interpreted this to refer to people who "hear the word and at once receive it with joy. But since they have no root, they last only a short time" (Mark 4:16–17). We may believe we have seen new life springing up within them, but under pressure, when they find out what it costs to follow Jesus Christ, they fall away. They wither and die because they haven't put their roots down into Him. Others in Jesus' parable found that new life crowded out by the concerns of their lives; everything else seems more important, and they fall away. In so doing, each proves that new life has never really taken root.

It is worth noting that in Hebrews 3:13 we are given some very fine advice about how to keep from falling away. The writer says, "Encourage one another daily, as long as it is called Today, so that none of you may be hardened by sin's deceitfulness." Part of sin's deceitfulness is to get you to believe that you can do this on your own. Of course you can't.

It is foolish to believe that we are capable of resisting sin and pleasing God on our own. We need, as this passage says, the accountability and the encouragement of the rest of the body of Christ if we are to avoid being deceived and ultimately destroyed by the distortions of our fallen world. The longer we live with those lies, the more our hearts are hardened and the less we are able to discern. If we are to survive, we need the stark challenge that the church provides to the subtle and deceitful lies of our culture. Indeed the suggestion here is that we need this support daily. We need each other's prayers, we need constantly to nurture our spirits if we are to continue in Jesus Christ. Otherwise those cultural weeds will simply crowd out the new life, and we will fall away; and in falling we will prove that Jesus is not in fact our Lord.

The emphasis on "today" in this verse underscores the all-important fact that right now, today, is the only time we can establish the pattern of behavior that demonstrates our commitment to Jesus Christ. You cannot change yesterday, because it is already past, and you cannot do anything about tomorrow, because it has not yet arrived. Both will be what you choose today. The person who rests on past laurels, or the person who promises to do better tomorrow, cannot please God. Today is the day that God evaluates in our lives. We fool ourselves in thinking we are going to do better tomorrow. The longer we put it off, the harder our hearts become and the more enmeshed we become in all those things that crowd out the life of God's Spirit in us.

The goal of this day-by-day encouragement in obedience is to save us from the subtle hardening of our hearts that sin so deceitfully accomplishes in us when we are not paying attention. Most of us do not set out blatantly to disregard God's Word. Sin deceives us into thinking, "Oh, this is just a little thing, a minor indulgence. It's really not all that serious." But, like the proverbial frog in the kettle, we don't notice the subtle degrees by which our resistance to sin is being melted away. Too late, we find ourselves so deeply entangled in sin that we are powerless to escape.

Since sin always leads to death, perseverance *cannot* mean that we can walk the path of sin and still have it lead to life. But if perseverance doesn't mean "once I'm saved, it doesn't matter what I do," what does it mean? According to the Scriptures, perseverance means that *the true believer will persevere in his faith*. That's how you can identify a true believer; he or she will persevere in following Christ. Not that true believers are guaranteed a place in heaven even if they fall away from following Christ, but rather that true believers won't stop following

Christ. They will persevere in following right up to the end. "We have come to share in Christ if we hold firmly till the end the confidence we had at first." That's what God's Word says.

WHAT PERSEVERANCE DOES MEAN

This is a critical distinction. The perseverance of the saints is no unconditional guarantee of our salvation. It is a guarantee that a true believer will continue to follow Christ. Anyone who does not continue to follow Christ proves in the end not to have been a true believer.

The apostle John wrote his first letter to help believers find a confidence or assurance that they really did have a place in God's family. He did not say, "Don't worry about it. If you call Jesus, 'Lord, Lord,' and repeat this little prayer, you'll be fine." Rather he said, "We know that we have come to know him *if we obey his commands.* The man who says, 'I know him,' but does not do what he commands is a liar. . . . This is how we know we are in him: *Whoever claims to live in him must walk as Jesus did*" (2:3–6, italics added). John goes on in verses 24–25 to give a classic definition of the perseverance of the saints. He says, "See that what you have heard from the beginning remains in you. If it does, you also will remain in the Son and in the Father. And this is what he promised us— even eternal life." If you continue to follow Him, He will not only take you to the border of the Promised Land, but He will take you in and establish you there. The true believer continues to walk with Jesus Christ right up until he enters the kingdom of heaven.

If you have been taking this seriously, you may be getting seriously worried about where you stand with

God. But there is a sense in which those who are seriously worried about this have the least to worry about. It's
those who aren't worried who ought to be worried. The
fact that you are concerned about your walk with Him
means that God's Spirit is active in your life. As long as
you continue to seek His face, He has promised to continue to be active within you. You will recognize the
presence of God's Spirit in your life by your concern
about following Christ and nurturing your relationship
with Him. But if you stop caring about that relationship,
then it's time to begin worrying, for there is no evidence
of the presence of God's Spirit in your life.

Those of us who are seriously concerned about sin
in our lives rightly ask, "Am I fooling myself about being
a Christian if I continue in sin?" But in this same letter,
John acknowledges, "If we claim to be without sin, we
deceive ourselves . . ." (We probably don't deceive anybody else, but we deceive ourselves.) On the other hand,
"If we confess our sins, he is faithful and just and will forgive us our sins and purify us from all unrighteousness"
(1 John 1:9). John goes on to say, "My dear children, I
write this to you so that you will not sin" (2:1). That must
be our goal. "But if anybody does sin, we have one who
speaks to the Father in our defense—Jesus Christ, the
Righteous One." A true believer grieves about his sin,
but rests in the knowledge that Jesus Christ is continually advocating for him before the throne of God.

CONSEQUENCES OF SIN FOR THE BELIEVER

The Westminster Confession points out (XVII.III)
that true believers may indeed fall rather deeply into sin
due to a number of factors: the intensity of the tempta-

tions we face, the corruption of sin that remains in us (it's hard to clean out all those bad habits we have established in our thinking and in our actions), or our neglect of the means of preservation (things like prayer and worship, the sacraments, and reading God's Word). In that sin, the Confession points out, we suffer many serious consequences: we incur God's displeasure; we grieve His Spirit; we deprive ourselves of many of His graces and comforts; we allow our own hearts to harden and make it more difficult to return; we hurt and scandalize others; we bring temporal judgments on ourselves.

Even if we are believers, much evil results from our sins. But the difference is, as John says in chapter 3 of his first letter, "No one who is born of God will continue to sin, because God's seed remains in him" (v. 9). The Spirit of God within you is making you uncomfortable with the sin in your life right now: "He cannot go on sinning because he has been born of God. This is how we know who the children of God are and who the children of the devil are" (vv. 9b–10). You understand, the children of God continue to work at the sin in their lives; the children of the devil don't. That's why true saints persevere.

King David, in the Old Testament, sinned grievously, and you know the result. It caused the death of a noble man, it scandalized those who looked to David as an example, and eventually it cost the life of his own infant son and of many of his subjects. But David came to recognize his sin, grieve over it, repent of it, and seek once again to be restored to a relationship with God. And that is why he is considered a man after God's own heart. He didn't prove to be a saint because he never sinned, but because even in the face of his sin, he persevered in pursuing a relationship with the Living God. That is the evidence that God's Spirit is alive in you. A true saint always perseveres. One who does not persevere is not a true saint.

We may at times find ourselves to be prodigal sons or daughters, who have rebelled and deliberately walked away from the Father's offer of a place in His family. If we do not return, then we are among those referred to in 1 John 2:19 who prove that we do not belong to God's family. But if, like the Prodigal Son, even in a far country, we finally come to our senses, recognize our sin, and in true repentance return to our Father, He acknowledges our true sonship at that moment by embracing us, placing the ring upon our finger, killing the fatted calf, and celebrating our return. This promise, however, is made only to those who do in fact return.

Personally, one of my great struggles grows out of my awareness that I am not really capable of living up to what God expects of me. I am not even capable of living up to what I expect of myself. I know beyond a doubt that, left to my own devices, eventually I would fall away from following Jesus Christ. I desperately need God's Spirit to sustain me in this life. As the Westminster Confession suggests, the temptations of the world are so strong, and the corruption of sin in my soul is so tenacious, and I am so often negligent in nurturing my relationship with God, that I am terribly vulnerable to sin. But since I know this, I have done the one thing I can do. I have committed my soul and my life into His hands. In awareness of my own shortcomings and my own weaknesses I have given myself to Him. Each day I have to get up and renew that commitment, not because I've lost my salvation overnight, but simply because surrender must be affirmed regularly or it is not surrender. I must continually come back to Him and declare my dependence upon Him.

As I do that, however, I receive a most wonderful assurance. I am reassured by His Spirit in me that He will accomplish what He has set out to accomplish. To the sheep who respond to His voice, Jesus says in John 10, He gives eternal life, "and they shall never perish; no one can snatch them out of my hand." You see, we are absolutely secure if we are in His hands! But we only know we are in His hands if we persevere.

WHY SAINTS PERSEVERE

Saints persevere, not because they are extraordinarily good, but because they are saints, and this is what God has planned for them. As Romans 8 says, having shaped us and known us in His sovereignty, "he predestined [us] to be conformed to the likeness of his Son" (v. 29). That is what God set out to do when He called you to belong to Him. He predetermined that one day you were going to be conformed to the image of His Son, and He is not going to give up on that job. He will continue to work until He accomplishes it. The passage goes on to say, "and those he predestined, he also called; those he called, he also justified; those he justified, he also glorified" (v. 30). Even glorification is so certain that He can say it in the past tense. That's what it means to have God's Spirit at work in your life. His will *will* be accomplished!

This is the wonderful promise of the perseverance of the saints. As it is something that God set out to do in us from the beginning, His plan cannot be frustrated. The apostle Paul says in that marvelously encouraging verse in Philippians 1:6, "Being confident of this, that he who began a good work in you will carry it on to completion until the day of Christ Jesus." It is right to be concerned about the times you stumble. But be reassured that if you have God's Spirit in your life—the One who keeps you sensitive to these concerns—He has begun a good work in you and He is going to bring it to completion in the day of Christ Jesus. It does not cease to demand your efforts, but the end result is entirely in His hands.

It is a beautiful promise! The job isn't done, but God promises that despite all our setbacks and frustrations, it will get done. When it gets done, it will be done right, and it will be done certainly because it will be the work of our Creator and Redeemer; it won't be restricted by our limitations.

We must not, however, neglect to cooperate with God in this matter. You remember Peter, the leader of the disciples. Like many of us, he was impetuous and made many rash declarations. He said, "Lord, Lord," and yet failed to follow through on his commitments. But he learned some things along the way. Perhaps he said it best in his second letter, where he spoke first of our potential:

> His divine power has given us everything we need for life and godliness through our knowledge of him who called us by his own glory and goodness. Through these he has given us his very great and precious promises, so that through them you may participate in the divine nature and escape the corruption in the world, caused by evil desires. (2 Peter 1:3–4)

This, he says, is what God has given us in His Spirit. When you acknowledge your helplessness and trust Jesus Christ as your Savior, He gives you *everything you need* to become conformed to His divine image and to escape the corruption of sin. *"But for this very reason,"* he goes on to say, you must not be passive. Rather, *"make every effort* to add to your faith goodness" (2 Peter 1:5, italics added). It is not enough to say, "Oh, I have faith!" "Make every effort to add to your faith goodness; and to goodness, knowledge; and to knowledge, self-control; and to self-control, perseverance; and to perseverance, godliness; and to godliness, brotherly kindness; and to brotherly kindness, love" (2 Peter 1:5–7). God has given you a potential you did not have before. But now it is up to you to work it out. Note the *process* implicit in the qualified promise:

> *For if you possess these qualities in increasing measure,* they will keep you from being ineffective and unproductive in your knowledge of our Lord Jesus Christ. But if anyone does not have them, he is nearsighted and blind, and has forgotten that he has been cleansed from his past sins.
>
> Therefore, my brothers, *be all the more eager to make your calling and election sure. For if you do these things, you will never fall,* and you will receive a rich welcome into the eternal kingdom of our Lord and Savior Jesus Christ. (2 Peter 1:8–11, italics added)

Many parents struggle with this on behalf of their children, and many of us struggle with it in our own lives. There is no question that the doctrine of the perseverance of the saints contains both a severe warning and a staggering promise. There is nothing assured in the sense that we can ever say, "There, that is done, I don't need to work at this any longer." We need to make a continuing effort, the Bible says, not because our effort is required to maintain our salvation, but because our effort demonstrates the genuineness of our faith, just as our failure to make an effort demonstrates the inauthenticity of our faith.

Yet all of us struggle with a vicious enemy here in this sin to which we are tempted. If we wander away, even to a far country, we will have to, one day, gather up the tattered remnants of our lives and return to the Father. We cannot put that off indefinitely. Indeed, the longer we wait, the more difficult it becomes, perhaps even to the point of impossibility. But we will not be forgiven and healed and restored until we do come back. And if we don't return, we prove that we never really trusted God in the first place, no matter what we said. We have chosen the course of trusting ourselves, instead of trusting Him.

In the end, the greatest thing we can do is pray. We can pray for our families and our loved ones and never stop praying. We can pray for each other. We can pray for ourselves. We can and should pray that we won't be reckless with sin and that we won't be presumptuous with God's grace. Perhaps the best thing that God does in our agony over wayward family members is keep *us* on our knees. Whatever He is doing in our children or our loved ones, He's doing something in us.

Finally, if you have heard the warning and the promise, don't ever underestimate God's mercy. We can have absolutely no assurance of His grace without our obedience. But He is, after all, in the business of redeeming sinners!

Chapter Eleven

THE COLONY

OF HEAVEN

Of the Community of Faith

Westminster Confession, chaps. XXV, XXVI;
1 Peter 2:4–12

*T*hose of you who are a part of a Christian congregation, do you have any idea who you are? A little band, perhaps, of kindly elderly folks; a nondescript bunch of working people wondering whether you will ever be secure in your careers; an assembly of struggling parents trying to do your best against enormous odds to raise your children as you believe you should; a distracted group of teenagers and young children waiting for a worship service to be over so you can go have some fun with your friends—do you know who you are?

Some of you come together for worship on a Sunday morning because it seems like the right thing to do, some because you haven't anything else to do, some because you feel so inadequate and need a bit of encouragement—do you really know why you are there? Look around you some Sunday morning. Look at the group of folks, large or small, with whom you worship. Would *you believe me if I told you that there is not a more important gathering of persons anywhere in the world than the persons gathered with you for worship?*

Likely you think I am exaggerating, but I'm not! As a pastor, sometimes I watch our nonchalant coming and going on a Sunday morning or hear the excuses for our failure to worship or to serve, and I think, "This is incredible! These people have no idea who they are. The whole of human history depends upon this gathering of people, and we haven't got a clue. God has set about bringing down the powers and principalities that have dominated and distorted His world for centuries; He has set in motion a plan that will culminate in the creation of new heavens and a new earth; these folks gathered in this room are the key to making all that happen—and we act as if nothing special is happening here on a Sunday morning!"

I am reminded of the prophet Samuel's admonition to Israel's first king, Saul: "Though you are little in your own eyes, are you not the head of the tribes of Israel? The Lord anointed you . . . and the Lord sent you on a mission. . . . Why then did you not obey the voice of the Lord?" (1 Samuel 15:17–19 RSV)

You and I may be little in our own eyes, but God has anointed us and sent us on the most significant mission in human history. As we consider the community of faith together, I want us to be overwhelmed with the importance of the little band of believers of which we are a part.[1]

GOD'S PLAN THROUGH THE AGES

When God saw His creation coming apart at the seams early on, He set out on a magnificent plan that would not only destroy the forces of evil undermining

His world, but would assure the triumph of all things good and beautiful. But it was not, as we might have anticipated, a plan to grab that world by the scruff of the neck and beat it into submission—something the Almighty God would have been capable of doing. Rather, He chose a particular man—really a very ordinary man not unlike any of us—and told him, "Abram, I want to bless you, and through you I want to bless all the peoples of the earth" (see Genesis 12:1–3).

He renewed that promise with Abraham's son Isaac and with his grandson Jacob. Then one day, after their descendants had suffered for several centuries as slaves in Egypt, He told Moses to say to them for Him,

> I am the LORD [Yahweh—the Source of all things], and I will bring you out from under the yoke of the Egyptians. I will free you from being slaves to them, and I will redeem you with an outstretched arm and with mighty acts of judgment. I will take you as my own people, and I will be your God. (Exodus 6:6–7)

And He did just that in a most spectacular way. But it was not, as we might have assumed, because these people were particularly special or talented or good. He had "set his affection on [them]" and chosen them, He explained later in Deuteronomy 7, simply because He wanted to! "I set my affection on you because I chose to love you" (see vv. 7–8), God says, beginning to sound a trifle redundant. In other words, "I love you because I choose to love you—not because you deserve it, but because I want to do it. It is My good pleasure to love you."

That little ragtag group was really clueless about what God was doing. The people went along with

Moses because they were slaves—they were used to doing what they were told. They scrambled away from their taskmasters in Egypt because there really was nothing else they could do under the circumstances; and the minute they had done it, they were terrified at what they had done and wanted to go back. But God had set out to do a great work with them in spite of their weakness and lack of courage. He had chosen them, and now He called them to come and meet with Him at Mount Sinai.

The Greek word for "church," *ekklesia,* is a translation of the Hebrew word *kahal,* which describes an assembly. This is not just a potential assembly, like a congregation that exists in theory whether anyone actually shows up or not. It describes an actual, physical gathering of people summoned for a purpose, and it is the word used here to describe the meeting God called with His people at Mount Sinai. Perhaps you remember the story from Exodus 19. There was thunder and lightning, the smoke billowed up from the mountain like a great cauldron, the mountain shook until the stones tumbled down its sides, there was a great blast from some preternatural trumpet which grew louder and louder, and then the voice of God spoke from the mountaintop.

What God said on that occasion was extraordinarily important. He said,

> You yourselves have seen what I did to Egypt, and how I carried you on eagles' wings and brought you to myself. Now if you obey me fully and keep my covenant, then out of all nations you will be my treasured possession. Although the whole earth is mine, you will be for me a kingdom of priests and a holy nation. (Exodus 19:4–6a)

God was saying, "You people whom I have called will be unique among all people." And He used a series of images—a treasured possession, a kingdom of priests, a holy nation—that will prove particularly significant in our study of the community of faith.

God had called out a people to belong to Himself. He chose them because He wanted to love them. He assembled them before Him and told them that He wanted them to be holy. But then came a most startling revelation. He—the Lord of the universe—wanted to dwell with them. If Moses would build a tabernacle there in the wilderness, the God who had created the universe would come and live in the midst of their camp and would accompany them wherever they went!

In no time, however, the people had reneged on their side of the agreement. They had rebelled against Him, and God said to Moses, "Leave this place . . . and go up to the land I promised on oath to Abraham, Isaac and Jacob. . . . I will send an angel before you. . . . But I will not go with you, because . . . I might destroy you on the way" (Exodus 33:1–3). As Edmund Clowney points out in his excellent volume *The Church,* the very thought threw Moses into despair. If God would not go with them, there was no point in going. "God at a safe distance was not enough."[2] "If your Presence does not go with us," Moses pleaded, "what else will distinguish [us] from all the other people on the face of the earth?" (vv. 15–16).

So God relented. The tabernacle was built, and God pitched His tent in the midst of the tribes of Israel. Later, when Solomon built the temple, God's glory filled it also with light and with power. Israel was utterly unique among all the peoples of the earth because God's presence lived with them.

Nevertheless, when the people forgot their calling to be His special possession, a people holy unto Him and a channel of His blessing to the world, His judgment fell severely upon them. Ezekiel watched in horror as the cloud of glory lifted from the temple and departed. What hope was there if God was not among them? But God was not finished with His people. He had made a promise, and He began to speak of a New Covenant under which He would transform the very hearts of His people. Isaiah in particular spoke of a coming Messiah:

> Here is my servant, whom I uphold, my chosen one in whom I delight; I will put my Spirit on him and he will bring justice to the nations. . . . I will . . . make you [that Messiah] to be a covenant for the people and a light for the Gentiles, to open eyes that are blind, to free captives from prison and to release from the dungeon those who sit in darkness. (Isaiah 42:1, 6b–7)

GOD'S PROPHESIED PLAN FULFILLED

And of course the Gospels resound with the delightful story of the birth of the Messiah, Jesus Christ, in fulfillment of that prophecy. He is identified with those prophetic names, "Wonderful Counselor, Mighty God, Everlasting Father, Prince of Peace." More to the point, His followers came to know Him by Isaiah's most revealing title, "Emmanuel"—God with us. The Lord had returned to dwell among His people.

Each of the gospel accounts begins with a description of the outpouring of God's Spirit upon the man

Jesus Christ. God's glory was no longer confined to a tent in the wilderness, or even a marble temple in Jerusalem. As the apostle Paul later wrote to the Colossians, "For God was pleased to have all his fullness dwell in him" (1:19), that is, in Jesus Christ. "Destroy this temple," Jesus said in John 2:19, "and I will raise it again in three days." The Jews, who were so sure that God, if He lived among His people at all, dwelt in that great stone edifice that had recently been erected in Jerusalem, didn't know what He was talking about. But God had come, you see, to dwell in their midst in a new temple now—the very body and spirit of Jesus Christ.

And Jesus immediately began to do what His Father had done before Him: He called individuals to Himself to be His disciples. "As the Father has loved me, so have I loved you," He said (John 15:9), explaining His reason for calling them. "You did not choose me, but I chose you and appointed you to go and bear fruit" (John 15:16). He would call not only His immediate circle of disciples, but also "I have other sheep that are not of this [fold]. I must bring them also" (John 10:16a). And with that promise He began to look ahead to the calling of us who stand at the threshold of the twenty-first century. "They too will listen to my voice.... My sheep listen to my voice; I know them, and they follow me" (John 10:16b, 27).

It was a new assembly, a new *ekklesia,* a gathering of those whom God had chosen, and who had responded to His call and were willing to become His disciples. "If anyone loves me," Jesus promised, "he will obey my teaching. My Father will love him, and we will come to him and make our home with him" (John 14:23). The parallels here are too obvious to overlook. In updating

His plan, God has once again called a people to belong to Him. He has assembled a new flock, challenged them to be holy, and promised to dwell in their presence. Indeed, He will be with them to the end of the age, provided they fulfill their calling to "make disciples" for Him among all peoples (Matthew 28:18–20).

But this too seemed about to fall apart. On the eve of His death by crucifixion, when Jesus revealed that He would be leaving His new disciples, they were as distressed as was Moses in the wilderness. The *promise,* you see, without the *presence* of God is too elusive. Without Him they could do nothing! But Jesus urged them not to be discouraged. If He went away, He would send His Holy Spirit to dwell, not simply *among* them, but, better by far, *within* them (John 14:16–17)! It was the ultimate promise first announced by the Old Testament prophets Jeremiah, Ezekiel, and Joel (Jeremiah 31:31; Ezekiel 36:26–27; Joel 2:28).

THE CLIMAX OF THE STORY

And this brings us to the climax of our story. This is where everything has been leading since the very beginning. Jesus' disciple Peter first saw the connection. In 1 Peter 2:4–5 he began to put the whole thing together. "As you come to him, the living Stone—rejected by men but chosen by God and precious to him—you also, like living stones, are being built into a spiritual house to be a holy priesthood." People stumble over this truth, he points out, but the truth is,

> You [believers] are a chosen people, a royal priesthood, a holy nation, a people belonging to God, that you may

declare the praises of him who called you out of darkness into his wonderful light. Once you were not a people, but now you are the people of God; once you had not received mercy, but now you have received mercy. (1 Peter 2:9–10)

Do you recognize those powerful images we first heard from the Lord as He spoke to His people on the slopes of Mount Sinai in Exodus 19? God had indeed chosen a people to call His own. He had assembled them before Him and charged them with holiness. He had promised to live among them, that in their uniqueness they might bear witness to the truth that could be a blessing to all people. That choice, that call to holiness, that promise of His presence was extended by Jesus to His disciples. And now it becomes evident that all these promises and challenges belong to us, the New Testament church. The Westminster Confession words it this way: "Unto this catholic visible church Christ hath given the ministry, oracles, and ordinances of God, for the gathering and perfecting of the saints" (XXV.III).

The apostle Paul wrote a thorough account of this community of believers in his letter to the Ephesians.

Praise be to the God and Father of our Lord Jesus Christ, who has blessed us . . . with every spiritual blessing. . . . For he chose us in him before the creation of the world to be holy and blameless in his sight. In love he predestined us to be adopted as his sons through Jesus Christ, . . . to the praise of his glorious grace. . . . Having believed, you were marked in him with a seal, the promised Holy Spirit, who is a deposit guaranteeing our inheritance. (Ephesians 1:3–6, 13)

Do you understand what this says about the church? We are, first of all, a *chosen* people! From before the creation of the world, God had in mind that we would belong to Him, and that we would be the instruments by which He dispensed His grace and His blessing to all the world. That's why He called us! We are, as Paul would explain to the Roman Christians (Romans 4:11–17), the spiritual children of Abraham—the family God intends to bless in order that we might in turn be a blessing.

Furthermore, He chose us to be *holy* and blameless in His sight, Ephesians 2:4 says. We are to be that holy nation, chosen and called to follow in the footsteps of Jesus. Once we were no people, but now we have been adopted as His children through Jesus Christ. According to the Confession, we "have fellowship with him in his graces, sufferings, death, resurrection, and glory" (XXVI.I).

"Consequently," Paul explained at the climax of Ephesians 2,

> you [that's us!] are no longer foreigners and aliens, but fellow citizens with God's people and members of God's household, built on the foundation of the apostles and prophets, with Christ Jesus himself as the chief cornerstone. In him the whole building is joined together and rises to become a holy temple in the Lord. And in him you too are being built together to become a dwelling in which God lives by his Spirit. (Ephesians 2:19–22)

As in the tabernacle in the wilderness, as in the Lord Jesus Christ Himself, God's Spirit lives within any gathering of believers who are known by His name!

Here is the ultimate expression of the community of believers. Our privilege is greater than that of the Old

Testament people of God; we are redeemed and purified in becoming disciples of Jesus Christ. But then came the truly remarkable development. Having dwelt among His people in the tabernacle of the Old Testament, and then in the person of Jesus Christ in the New, God now extends Himself through His Spirit to live within believers themselves. In the fullest sense, we become the fellowship of the Holy Spirit.

God's Word reveals all kinds of things about who we are in that fellowship:

(1) We are, first of all, a community. Evangelicals often struggle with this, but the Bible knows nothing of "born-again individuals." We have been so intent on discrediting the Catholic notion of "no salvation apart from the church" that we fail to see the truth that the Reformers saw, namely, that from the beginning, God has always called His people into a family or a community where they share a mutual responsibility (XXVI.I, II). It is true that the church does not have the authority to dispense salvation. But it is also true that any Christian who is not attached to the body of Christ has as much chance of surviving and thriving as does an eye or a foot or a lung that has been detached from the body. That is what it means to be attached to the body of Jesus Christ.

(2) Not only are we a community, but that community is founded upon Jesus Christ. He is the chief cornerstone. Each of us becomes a part of the church the moment we are joined to Him. In union with Jesus Christ, of course, we share His life, which means we will share His sufferings as well as His resurrection.

(3) Furthermore, in union with Christ, we find ourselves in communion with all other believers. John

wrote that his proclamation of the gospel was intended to bring us into fellowship with other believers who, in turn, were enjoying fellowship with God the Father and with His Son, Jesus Christ (1 John 1:1–3).

(4) Not separately, but together we become a dwelling place for God's Holy Spirit, as both Peter and Paul proclaimed. God Himself comes to live with us in the true church.

There is, of course, tremendous value to this design. As we bring our particular gifts and abilities, distributed to us by the Holy Spirit, we are equipped to build each other up (cf. 1 Corinthians 12; Ephesians 4:11–16). This is the way God strengthens individual believers. In the community of believers too we find the courage to stand apart from a world that viciously defends political correctness and mocks anyone who takes issue with the world's distorted norms. Furthermore, community expresses what is fundamental to our calling. We are not one of "a thousand points of light." Jesus calls us "a city set on a hill." In a fragmented world where brother is set against brother and sister against sister, the Christian community should demonstrate by its very life that God is doing a work of grace in this place.

There is so much more we might say about the church. We could speak of the life-transforming power released by God's Spirit in us, of the privileges of membership in His family, of the commission to be a blessing to others.

But let us conclude with a final insight into this remarkable community of which every true believer is a part. We are the *ekklesia,* the assembly of those God has called to belong to Him. That first call to assemble at

Mount Sinai in the wilderness hardly anticipated the community that was to follow. Hebrews 12:18–24 spells it out in a magnificent way:

> You have not come to a mountain that can be touched and that is burning with fire; to darkness, gloom and storm; to a trumpet blast or to such a voice speaking words . . . [a] sight so terrifying that Moses said, "I am trembling with fear." But you have come to Mount Zion, to the heavenly Jerusalem, the city of the living God. You have come to thousands upon thousands of angels in joyful assembly, to the church of the firstborn, whose names are written in heaven. You have come to God . . . to the spirits of righteous men made perfect, to Jesus the mediator of a new covenant.

Understand, the communion of saints includes far more than the community of true believers that stretches around the globe today. The communion of saints includes all the saints in history, from Adam to Abraham to Moses and David and Elijah. It includes Peter and Paul and John and Barnabas. It includes St. Augustine and Luther and Calvin; Hudson Taylor and Dwight L. Moody. And if that is not enough, the "assembly" of God includes, according to the writer of Hebrews, the very hosts of heaven, the angels in all their glory, and God Himself, with His Son Jesus Christ.

If our worship in our singular congregations on a Sunday morning seems small or insignificant to you, keep in mind it is only because we are an outpost of heaven. We are a tiny colony in an alien land, but we have been placed here by the Lord of the universe Himself. And we have been placed here for a purpose. That purpose is to reflect in this world of darkness and despair the light and the hope and the promise and the joy of the City of God, the New Jerusalem, which will be our true homeland when our Lord recalls us with the words, "Well done, good and faithful servant! . . . Come and share your master's happiness!"

NOTES

1. The story which follows of God's presence in the gathering of His people grew originally out of our Inquirer's class. However, recently I discovered that Edmund P. Clowney in his book, *The Church, Contours of Christian Theology* (Downers Grove, Ill.: InterVarsity, 1995) had said this about as well as it can be said. I owe him an enormous debt in the inspiration of this chapter.
2. Clowney, *The Church,* 32.

Chapter Twelve

DARKNESS

BEFORE DAWN

Of the Final Judgment

Westminster Confession, chaps. XXXII, XXXIII;
2 Peter 3:1–13

*D*avid sat motionless behind the wheel of his car in the darkness, waiting for the light to change. A cold rain coursed down the windshield, only momentarily interrupted by the rhythmic passing of the wiper blades. But David could not wipe away the image of the dying man he had just visited in the hospital. The rhythmic click and hiss of the respirator echoed in his ears, and he could see the white face of the patient, as well as the dark circles under the eyes of the man's wife, who was sitting in the shadows of the darkened room. They were not believers; they had no hope; they were facing death, and David knew that, despite society's cavalier disregard for such "antiquated" doctrines as the final judgment, this man was about to find out for himself what it was all about.

As a pastor, David had long ago recognized the staggering implications of our belief in life after death and a God who takes seriously our conduct in this life. *Those who deny it are in the end left with a trivial universe perhaps best described by the atheist philosopher, Bertrand Russell: "There is darkness without, and when I die there will be darkness within. There is no splendour, no vastness anywhere; only triviality for a moment, and then nothing." But if he is wrong, if life is more than that, it can only be because there truly is a God who cares about who we are, a God who cares about how we live, and a God who meets us, for better or for worse, at the threshold of death.*

The Westminster Confession concludes with a troubling look at the doctrine of the final judgment, a doctrine scoffed at by the skeptics of our day, but clearly and powerfully taught by Jesus Christ, whom we acknowledge as the Author and Finisher of our faith. It says,

> God hath appointed a day, wherein he will judge the world, in righteousness, by Jesus Christ, to whom all power and judgment is given of the Father. In which day . . . all persons that have lived upon earth shall appear before the tribunal of Christ, to give an account of their thoughts, words, and deeds; and to receive according to what they have done in the body, whether good or evil. (XXXIII.I)

It is not, at first glance, a particularly appealing doctrine, but it is indispensable to our ultimate Christian hope. I want to walk us through this doctrine with a rather dramatic outline: (1) Descending darkness, (2) longing for the morning, (3) the fire falls, and (4) all things made new. This will give us a vivid image of the necessary progression through judgment to the glorious dawning of a new and perfect day in Christ Jesus.

THE DESCENDING DARKNESS OF OUR WORLD

Years ago when my wife and I were still young and foolish (today we are simply old and foolish), we were camping one summer in the Big Horn Mountains of Wyoming with a tiny, single-walled nylon tent about six feet long (which is not as long as I am). As we approached the mountains that day, we could see giant thunderclouds boiling up over the jagged peaks. The clouds eventually obscured the sun and enveloped us in a descending darkness. Undeterred, however, we pitched our little tent under towering evergreens near the summit in preparation for spending the night on Bald Mountain. We were about to learn something of the terror the Russian composer Modest Mussorgsky reflected in his orchestral work by the same name, *Night on Bald Mountain.*

Sometime around midnight, as we lay beneath the thin walls of our tent listening to the approaching storm, we began to wish rather desperately that it were already morning. But the worst was yet to come. With a brilliant flash of lightning and the deafening roar of thunder, the skies opened up and the tempest struck with a terrifying fury. For several hours the fire fell from heaven and torrents of rain invaded our tent, prompting us to wonder whether the world would finally end in fire or flood. But eventually the morning dawned with a freshness and beauty that simply took our breath away at ten thousand feet on Bald Mountain. The world had been renewed during the night through the storm, and we, best of all, had survived to enjoy it.

One cannot look honestly at our world today and fail to see the descending darkness. The apostle Paul, among others, predicted it. In his second letter to Timothy he warned,

> But mark this: There will be terrible times in the last days. People will be lovers of themselves, lovers of money, boastful, proud, abusive, disobedient to their parents, ungrateful, unholy, without love, unforgiving, slanderous, without self-control, brutal, not lovers of the good, treacherous, rash, conceited, lovers of pleasure rather than lovers of God—having a form of godliness but denying its power. (2 Timothy 3:1–5)

This well describes the growing trends in our day. We see increasing immorality, superficiality in our culture, self-indulgence, preoccupation with our own pleasure, and lack of character and integrity—blatant in our leaders but unchallenged because it is so characteristic of ourselves. We see increasing hostility toward the Christian faith; a rise in violent, self-serving fundamentalism in many religions across the world's face; a debilitating polarization of our society; and increasingly destructive technological capability that makes this all the more serious to contemplate. Are we indeed, as Robert Bork persuasively suggests, "slouching towards Gomorrah"? Does the descending darkness in our society portend the judgment of a holy God?

Scoffers, of course, as Peter points out in his second letter, are bound to reply blithely that things aren't going to change. They will claim, "Ever since our fathers died, everything goes on as it has since the beginning of creation" (3:3–4). That is a reference to what is known in scientific circles as the uniformity of natural causes in a closed system. We don't believe there is a god to interfere. The world will go on as usual. Hopefully it will renew itself.

With or without a god, of course, we are increasingly aware of the vulnerability of life on this planet. Nuclear holocaust, experiments in biological warfare gone amok, or the disruption of the fragile balance of our life-support system on this planet could trigger a devastating crisis at least as threatening as Noah's Flood of old. But that example brings us back to the more critical point. If the Flood was a natural disaster, albeit of unparalleled proportions, the salient point is that God did it on purpose! It was God's response, as He pointed out in Genesis 6:5–7, to the grievous behavior of the human race. It was brought about by the word of the God who had created the earth by the power of His word and who can as easily destroy it with a word. Indeed, He has already warned us, as Peter points out (2 Peter 3:7), that a judgment by fire is pending in response to our ungodly behavior. What we see around us today is not at all unlike the conduct of the people in Noah's day. In the gathering darkness of our world, we can easily see how God may be, as He was in the days of Noah, "grieved that he had made man on the earth," seeing as how our hearts are equally inclined toward evil all the time.

Once again, scoffers among us will say, there is nothing new about the conduct of the human race. It has always been this way. One can find throughout history and literature recurring references to the abysmal decline of morals and civil behavior. ("What is this world coming to?") True. But people deliberately ignore the fact that a holy God cannot overlook evil indefinitely. He may delay His judgment; He will not overlook it forever.

Indeed, in one sense history *is* cyclical. Reform follows decline, and civilization is saved from annihilation.

It may happen again in our day. But two things are different today, and they cause us to take careful note of the situation in our world. One is the potential scope of disaster in our technologically advanced world. We can do so much more damage than we have ever been capable of doing in human history. The other, more to the point here, is that according to God's Word, up to now Satan has been *restricted* in the extent to which he can do evil in our world. We have a window in human history in the last days during which the Great Commission is to be fulfilled, but there is coming a day when Satan will be allowed to deceive the nations and to cause untold destruction as evil is released to become as bad as it is capable of being. We all know the potential for evil has been restrained in our world. People who are not believers still do good things because God's Spirit is at work in our world. But when that Spirit finally withdraws and evil is allowed its day, God's judgment will fall.

THE LONGING FOR THE MORNING

In the midst of that gathering darkness, good people long for the morning. How do we explain mankind's longing for what is good? That is a philosophical question with practical implications. Something deep in the heart of every human being longs for a better world. For all our attempts to justify our own behavior, we desire something better. We desire a world where people *do* keep their word, even though we so very often don't keep our own. We desire a world where generosity and selflessness displace self-indulgence, even though we spend a lot of time indulging ourselves. We desire a world where people wisely use the magnificent resources and protect the beauty of our planet, a world where violence and distortion and pain have been eliminated, and where all things live in harmony.

How is it that we have such a strong sense that certain things "ought to be"—certain things that we have never seen in the history of the world and things we are not inclined to do ourselves? C. S. Lewis has persuasively argued that in a strictly naturalistic world, without any input from God, we could only have a sense of what *is,* not what *ought to be.* That awful night on Bald Mountain, my wife and I could only hope for the morning because we had known morning. Had we never known anything but the darkness and the storm, we could not have anticipated anything more. Likewise the idea of a moral world freed of all distortion, the idea of what the world *should* look like if it weren't broken, is an idea that comes from God. How would we know distortion if we didn't know the ideal?

But if a God exists who desires a world from which all evil has been eliminated, we had better believe that He will ultimately bring that about. He will not sit wringing His hands and saying, "Oh, I wish things were different!" A sovereign God is capable of accomplishing what He wills. "My word," He says through the prophet Isaiah, "will not return to me empty, but will accomplish what I desire" (Isaiah 55:11). And what He desires is a world made holy and pure once again. To achieve that He must remove all that is impure and unholy. Thus our very longing for the morning anticipates the purging judgment that is essential to prepare for the dawning of that last great day!

Recognizing that God wants to make all things

right, we may ask why He doesn't get on with it. Why is there such a delay? Thousands of years have gone by since Peter wrote. Why has God not accomplished what He set out to do? The answer, as Peter explains, is that God, knowing the awful truth about judgment—a judgment we cannot fathom—delays in order to give us opportunity to repent (2 Peter 3:9). He says in effect, "Trust Me; you don't want to have to face this. You need to think seriously about where you stand."

For the moment, Satan is limited in his ability to wreak havoc, allowing an opportunity for the gospel to go out to all the earth, and for all people everywhere to respond to God's offer of grace before the end comes and evil is unleashed (cf. Matthew 24:15–35). Accepting God's grace before the judgment falls is essential, since the evil and impurity He will judge do not exist in the abstract. Those terms describe our own conduct when it veers from God's norm. The simple fact is that *we* are the source of evil and impurity in this world. We are those whose conduct may be described as unholy and impure. Thus, if God is going to get rid of unholiness and impurity, it is we who are in jeopardy. As pointed out in chapter 6, repentance, turning away from our wicked ways, is essential to escaping the judgment we deserve. Jesus Christ suffered the wrath of God against sin on our behalf, but unless we turn from our wicked ways to follow Him, we cannot be healed.

THE FIRE FALLS

So the Lord delays, but in the gathering darkness we are fools if we ignore the certain signs of the impending storm. Peter describes the holocaust. First he says, "But the day of the Lord will come like a thief." Consistently God's judgment is presented as a sudden, unexpected event. "The heavens will disappear with a roar; the elements will be destroyed by fire, and the earth and everything in it will be laid bare" (2 Peter 3:10). Make no mistake; when the fire falls, it will be absolutely devastating.

"Then suddenly the Lord you are seeking will come to his temple," the prophet Malachi warns, "but who can endure the day of his coming? Who can stand when he appears? For he will be like a refiner's fire or a launderer's soap" (Malachi 3:1–2). This is the purging effect that God intends as the result of His judgment. Like a refiner's fire it will burn away the dross and the impurities in His world; like lye, it will burn away the harmful contaminants of His world and cleanse it to make it holy and pure once again.

We need to understand a number of things about the judgment that God has promised will precede the great climax of history. The first is that Jesus Christ is Himself the judge. "The Father judges no one, but has entrusted all judgment to the Son," Jesus explained in John 5:22. "Do not be amazed at this," He went on, "for a time is coming when all who are in their graves will hear his voice and come out—those who have done good will rise to live, and those who have done evil will rise to be condemned" (John 5:28–29). Those are the words of Jesus. Life does *not* end with annihilation, as many who are unprepared to meet God would like to believe. There is *not* a moment of triviality and then nothing, as Bertrand Russell says. Jesus says there will be a day when each person will arise to meet the Lord.

The second thing to know is that the entire human

race will be judged at that time. In Jesus' memorable description of the final judgment in Matthew 25:31–46, He says, "When the Son of Man comes in his glory ... all the nations will be gathered before him, and he will separate the people one from another as a shepherd separates the sheep from the goats." All of us are included—peoples of all nations, whatever our religious background, whatever our thoughts or philosophies of life. Judgment is not reserved only for criminals or pagans. It's for all of us.

The third thing to know is that we will be judged according to our deeds. This is a confusing thing for Christians to accept, as we have been nurtured on the fundamental truth of salvation by grace through faith alone. But we must not forget that it was Jesus Himself who warned, "For the Son of Man is going to come in his Father's glory with his angels, and then he will reward each person *according to what he has done*" (Matthew 16:27, italics added). In Matthew 25, what was the critical issue at stake in Christ's judgment? Read the passage. What caused Him to distinguish between the sheep and the goats? The answer, surprisingly, is not our beliefs but our conduct! Of course we could never earn our salvation. We have learned that by now. Christ's death on the cross won our salvation for us. But the question Jesus asks is whether the way we lived our lives, the way we treated other people, reflected the grace and the truth of Jesus Christ. Nowhere in Scripture will you find that faith makes works irrelevant. On the contrary, the connection is so strong that Jesus suggests our conduct will unerringly reveal our hearts.

Even our casual conversation is subject to the scrutiny of a holy God. To the Pharisees He said, "Men will have to give account on the day of judgment for every careless word they have spoken. For by your words you will be acquitted, and by your words you will be condemned" (Matthew 12:36–37).

The apostle Paul warns that when the Lord comes to judge, "He will bring to light what is hidden in darkness and will expose the motives of men's hearts" (1 Corinthians 4:5). (It's disconcerting enough that you should see what I have actually done. Suppose you should see what is in my heart!) "Each of us," he tells the Roman Christians, "will give an account of himself to God" (Romans 14:12). And to the Corinthians he explains, "For we must all appear before the judgment seat of Christ, that each one may receive what is due him for the things done while in the body, whether good or bad" (2 Corinthians 5:10).

You may say, "I thought we weren't judged by works. I thought we were judged by grace." But remember what we said about faith and works in chapter 9? Our works demonstrate whether or not we have faith. If we truly have faith in God, then there will be a difference in our lives. God's Spirit will be transforming us. It *does* make a difference how we live our lives.

Finally, judgment involves not an equalizing of all people and all deeds, but a stark division between those who end up at Christ's right hand with an invitation to share the joy and blessing of the King, and those at His left hand who are told, "Depart from me, you who are cursed, into the eternal fire prepared for the devil and his angels" (Matthew 25:41). In this day of undiscerning tolerance and irrational egalitarianism, characterized by our obsession with treating everyone precisely the same regardless of conduct or mitigating circumstances, we don't like to hear that God might treat people differently. But that is the fundamental idea of His judgment as Jesus Himself describes it.

Throughout the Gospels this division is apparent. To His disciples Jesus explained that in that moment of judgment, two would be working in the field or grinding at the mill, "one will be taken and the other left" (Matthew 24:40–41). God has discriminated between them. Of the ten virgins waiting for the bridegroom, five were prepared and five were not prepared. Those unprepared were simply shut out of the banquet (Matthew 25:1–13). And Jesus said that is the way it will be in the final day.

In *The Jesus Hope,* Stephen Travis points out, "It will be no use protesting that God ought to have given us a 'second chance' after death."[1] He says God is *continually* offering us chances to respond to His love. It wouldn't be a second chance anyway; it would be a hundredth, it would be a thousandth, it would be a ten thousandth! We've had plenty of opportunities to respond. C. S. Lewis reminds us that we must grow out of a fairy-tale attitude that says everything will turn out all right in the end. We live in a *real* world with *real* choices to be made. And the way we choose will determine whether our lives move toward blessing or disaster.

As the Westminster Confession points out (XXXIII. III), knowing that the fire will one day fall, whether we are prepared or not, should be incentive for us to be prepared: to surrender to Jesus Christ and to avoid sin in our lives, in order that we might be assured of receiving Christ's blessing instead of His judgment. But whether or not God's reminder of the certainty of judgment is incentive for us to avoid sin, there is a positive side to the story of judgment as well. In addition to warning, it is a source of great hope. For the wonderful thing we must all recognize about the final judgment is that it is not the final act of God. Christians should not be doomsayers who point accusing fingers and warn with morbid delight about the fires of hell. The story of the final judgment is ultimately the story of a delightful universe in which all things are made new.

ALL THINGS MADE NEW

That dark judgment of which Jesus and the gospel writers so often speak is the darkness that precedes the dawn. It is the storm that cleanses the whole earth, along with the hearts of truly penitent men and women, so that God can restore "a new heaven and a new earth in which righteousness dwells"—the sort of place for which our hearts have longed from the beginning. This judgment touches not only each of us but our world as well. Paul says in Romans 8:19–25 that the whole of creation is waiting with eager longing for that day when we are finally set right with God, so that creation too may be renewed.

Peter spoke of this new heaven and new earth, and it is the dominant theme of the book of Revelation. It was first described by Isaiah the prophet, in the Old Testament. Through Isaiah God said, "Behold, I will create new heavens and a new earth. The former things will not be remembered, nor will they come to mind. But be glad and rejoice forever in what I will create" (65:17–18). Then he goes on to describe a place of joy and health and harmony where "the sound of weeping and of crying will be heard in it no more" (v. 19b), and where "the wolf and the lamb will feed together, and the lion will eat straw like the ox, . . . [and] they will neither harm nor destroy on all my holy mountain" (v. 25).

In his Revelation, John spoke excitedly of this place where God Himself would dwell in the midst of His people once again, as He had at the tabernacle in the wilderness, illuminated by the Shekinah glory. And He Himself, personally, would "wipe every tear from their eyes. There will be no more death or mourning or crying or pain, for the old order of things has passed away." That is what we can look forward to after that final judgment! The old order of things has passed away (Revelation 21:4). "Behold," Jesus says, "I am making all things new" (v. 5 NASB).

Evil, too, will be gone, the book of Revelation says, for "nothing impure will ever enter it, nor will anyone who does what is shameful or deceitful, but only those whose names are written in the Lamb's book of life" (v. 27) —that's the book in which our names are written when, in response to Christ's call, we declare our allegiance to Him as Lord. Understand, that is the only way we can escape the judgment. Christ has already suffered that judgment for us. And when we are united with Jesus Christ, when we are bound to Him and made one with Him in our declaration of faith in Him, we are brought through the judgment to that place He has prepared for His loved ones.

In the end, what God's Word describes beyond the final judgment is a transformed universe! Isaiah began his famous description of a world in which even the animals are transformed with the Hebrew word *bara'*. It is the powerful word used in Genesis 1 to describe the way God brought the world into being by the power of His word. Thus he says, "Behold, I will *create* new heavens *and a new earth*" (Isaiah 65:17, italics added). Paul says in Romans 8 that "creation itself will be liberated from its bondage to decay and brought into the glorious freedom of the children of God." Peter looks forward to "a new heaven and a new earth, the home of righteousness" to be established after the purging fires of judgment (2 Peter 3:13). And of course John in Revelation 21 described a new heaven and a new earth offered to believers as the place where they may dwell eternally with God, free from the suffering that has characterized our fallen world.

Many Christians envision themselves living for eternity in some ethereal heaven, and many pagans reject heaven for the elusive joys of earth that seem much more enticing. But what the Bible describes is not simply a heaven far off someplace, but a renewed earth. A whole new earth as well as an unimaginable heaven beyond! I believe with all my heart that in that great final judgment, God intends to salvage everything that is good in His creation. It is not going to be gone; it's going to be renewed. Having freed it from the pollution of our sin, He will establish a universe so full of delight that the Garden of Eden, for which we have longed since the dawn of creation, will serve simply as an entryway. You will walk in and say, "This is delightful! But there is more beyond."

To many this description will seem naive and idealistic, hopelessly out of touch with the real world. But on the word of my Lord Jesus Christ, I have simply described to you what He has promised. These are not my words; they are His. If you are willing to take *Him* at His word, you may enjoy that promise as well. It seems more likely that those who are unwilling to take the word of the Creator of the universe on these matters are the ones who are out of touch. Those locked into the material world that is passing away are in touch with a shadow world, not the real world He is in the process of renewing and remaking. Jesus did not die that the universe might remain in its brokenness. Jesus died that He might make all things new. Even so, as the Westminster Confession ends, "Come, Lord Jesus, come quickly!"

NOTE

1. Stephen Travis, *The Jesus Hope* (Downers Grove, Ill.: InterVarsity, 1974), 66.

THE WESTMINSTER
CONFESSION OF FAITH

CHAPTER I
Of the Holy Scripture

I. Although the light of nature, and the works of creation and providence do so far manifest the goodness, wisdom, and power of God, as to leave men unexcusable; yet are they not sufficient to give that knowledge of God, and of his will, which is necessary unto salvation. Therefore it pleased the Lord, at sundry times, and in divers manners, to reveal himself, and to declare that his will unto his church; and afterwards, for the better preserving and propagating of the truth, and for the more sure establishment and comfort of the church against the corruption of the flesh, and the malice of Satan and of the world, to commit the same wholly unto writing: which maketh the holy Scripture to be most necessary; those former ways of God's revealing his will unto his people being now ceased.

II. Under the name of holy Scripture, or the Word of God written, are now contained all the books of the Old and New Testaments, which are these:

Of the Old Testament:

Genesis	*II Chronicles*	*Daniel*
Exodus	*Ezra*	*Hosea*
Leviticus	*Nehemiah*	*Joel*
Numbers	*Esther*	*Amos*
Deuteronomy	*Job*	*Obadiah*
Joshua	*Psalms*	*Jonah*
Judges	*Proverbs*	*Micah*
Ruth	*Ecclesiastes*	*Nahum*
I Samuel	*The Song of Songs*	*Habakkuk*
II Samuel	*Isaiah*	*Zephaniah*
I Kings	*Jeremiah*	*Haggai*
II Kings	*Lamentations*	*Zechariah*
I Chronicles	*Ezekiel*	*Malachi*

Of the New Testament:

The Gospels according to
Matthew
Mark
Luke
John
The Acts of the Apostles

Paul's Epistles to
the Romans
the Corinthians I
the Corinthians II
the Galatians
the Ephesians
the Philippians
the Colossians
the Thessalonians I
the Thessalonians II

Timothy I
Timothy II
Titus
Philemon
The Epistle to the Hebrews
The Epistle of James
The first and second Epistles of Peter
The first, second, and third Epistles of John
The Epistle of Jude
The Revelation of John

All which are given by inspiration of God to be the rule of faith and life.

III. The books commonly called *Apocrypha,* not being of divine inspiration, are no part of the canon of the Scripture, and therefore are of no authority in the church of God, nor to be any otherwise approved, or made use of, than other human writings.

IV. The authority of the holy Scripture, for which it ought to be believed, and obeyed, dependeth not upon the testimony of any man, or church; but wholly upon God (who is truth itself) the author thereof: and therefore it is to be received, because it is the Word of God.

V. We may be moved and induced by the testimony of the church to an high and reverent esteem of the holy Scripture. And the heavenliness of the matter, the efficacy of the doctrine, the majesty of the style, the consent of all the parts, the scope of the whole (which is, to give all glory to God), the full discovery it makes of the only way of man's salvation, the many other incomparable excellencies, and the entire perfection thereof, are arguments whereby it doth abundantly evidence itself to be the Word of God: yet notwithstanding, our full persuasion and assurance of the infallible truth and divine authority thereof, is from the inward work of the Holy Spirit bearing witness by and with the Word in our hearts.

VI. The whole counsel of God concerning all things necessary for his own glory, man's salvation, faith and life, is either expressly set down in Scripture, or by good and necessary consequence may be deduced from Scripture: unto which nothing at any time is to be added, whether by new revelations of the Spirit, or traditions of men. Nevertheless, we acknowledge the inward illumination of the Spirit of God to be necessary for the saving understanding of such things as are revealed in the Word: and that there are some circumstances concerning the worship of God, and government of the church, common to human actions and societies, which are to be ordered by the light of nature, and Christian prudence, according to the general rules of the Word, which are always to be observed.

VII. All things in Scripture are not alike plain in themselves, nor alike clear unto all: yet those things which are necessary to be known, believed, and observed for salvation, are so clearly propounded, and opened in some place of Scripture or other, that not only the learned, but the unlearned, in a due use of the ordinary means, may attain unto a sufficient understanding of them.

VIII. The Old Testament in Hebrew (which was the native language of the people of God of old), and the New Testament in Greek (which, at the time of the writing of it, was most generally known to the nations), being immediately inspired by God, and, by his singular care and providence, kept pure in all ages, are therefore authentical; so as, in all controversies of religion, the church is finally to appeal unto them. But, because these original tongues are not known to all the people of God, who have right unto, and interest in the Scriptures, and are commanded, in the fear of God, to read and search them, therefore they are to be translated into the vulgar language of every nation unto which they come, that, the Word of God dwelling plentifully in all, they may worship him in an acceptable manner; and, through patience and comfort of the Scriptures, may have hope.

IX. The infallible rule of interpretation of Scripture is the Scripture itself: and therefore, when there is a question about the true and full sense of any Scripture (which is not manifold, but one), it must be searched and known by other places that speak more clearly.

X. The supreme judge by which all controversies of religion are to be determined, and all decrees of councils, opinions of ancient writers, doctrines of men, and private spirits, are to be examined, and in whose sentence we are to rest, can be no other but the Holy Spirit speaking in the Scripture.

CHAPTER II
Of God and of the Holy Trinity

I. There is but one only, living, and true God, who is infinite in being and perfection, a most pure spirit, invisible, without body, parts, or passions; immutable, immense, eternal, incomprehensible, almighty, most wise, most holy, most free, most absolute; working all things according to the counsel of his own immutable and most righteous will, for his own glory; most loving, gracious, merciful, long-suffering, abundant in goodness and truth, forgiving iniquity, transgression, and sin; the rewarder of them that diligently seek him; and withal, most just, and terrible in his judgments, hating all sin, and who will by no means clear the guilty.

II. God hath all life, glory, goodness, blessedness, in and of himself; and is alone in and unto himself all-sufficient, not standing in need of any creatures which he hath made, nor deriving any glory from them, but only manifesting his own glory in, by, unto, and upon them. He is the alone fountain of all being, of whom, through whom, and to whom are all things; and hath most sovereign dominion over them, to do by them, for them, or upon them whatsoever himself pleaseth. In his sight all things are open and manifest, his knowledge is infinite, infallible, and independent upon the creature, so as nothing is to him contingent, or uncertain. He is most holy in all his counsels, in all his works, and in all his commands. To him is due from angels and men, and every other creature, whatsoever worship, service, or obedience he is pleased to require of them.

III. In the unity of the Godhead there be three persons, of one substance, power, and eternity: God the Father, God the Son, and God the Holy Ghost: the Father is of none, neither begotten, nor proceeding; the Son is eternally begotten of the Father; the Holy Ghost eternally proceeding from the Father and the Son.

CHAPTER III
Of God's Eternal Decree

I. God, from all eternity, did, by the most wise and holy counsel of his will, freely, and unchangeably ordain whatsoever comes to pass: yet so, as thereby neither is God the author of sin, nor is violence offered to the will of the creatures; nor is the liberty or contingency of second causes taken away, but rather established.

II. Although God knows whatsoever may or can come to pass upon all supposed conditions, yet hath he not decreed anything because he foresaw it as future, or as that which would come to pass upon such conditions.

III. By the decree of God, for the manifestation of his glory, some men and angels are predestinated unto everlasting life; and others foreordained to everlasting death.

IV. These angels and men, thus predestinated, and foreordained, are particularly and unchangeably designed, and their number so certain and definite, that it cannot be either increased or diminished.

V. Those of mankind that are predestinated unto life, God, before the foundation of the world was laid, according to his eternal and immutable purpose, and the secret counsel and good pleasure of his will, hath chosen, in Christ, unto everlasting glory, out of his mere free grace and love, without any foresight of faith, or good works, or perseverance in either of them, or any other thing in the creature, as conditions, or causes moving him thereunto; and all to the praise of his glorious grace.

VI. As God hath appointed the elect unto glory, so hath he, by the eternal and most free purpose of his will, foreordained all the means thereunto. Wherefore, they who are elected, being fallen in Adam, are redeemed by Christ, are effectually called unto faith in Christ by his Spirit working in due season, are justified, adopted, sanctified, and kept by his power, through faith, unto salvation. Neither are any other redeemed by Christ, effectually called, justified, adopted, sanctified, and saved, but the elect only.

VII. The rest of mankind God was pleased, according to the unsearchable counsel of his own will, whereby he extendeth or withholdeth mercy, as he pleaseth, for the glory of his sovereign power over his creatures, to pass by; and to ordain them to dishonor and wrath for their sin, to the praise of his glorious justice.

VIII. The doctrine of this high mystery of predestination is to be handled with special prudence and care, that men, attending the will of God revealed in his Word, and yielding obedience thereunto, may, from the certainty of their effectual vocation, be assured of their eternal election. So shall this doctrine afford matter of praise, reverence, and admiration of God; and of humility, diligence, and abundant consolation to all that sincerely obey the gospel.

CHAPTER IV
Of Creation

I. It pleased God the Father, Son, and Holy Ghost, for the manifestation of the glory of his eternal power, wisdom, and goodness, in the beginning, to create, or make of nothing, the world, and all things therein whether visible or invisible, in the space of six days; and all very good.

II. After God had made all other creatures, he created man, male and female, with reasonable and immortal souls, endued with knowledge, righteousness, and true holiness, after his own image; having the law of God written in their hearts, and power to fulfil it: and yet under a possibility of transgressing, being left to the liberty of their own will, which was subject unto change. Beside this law written in their hearts, they received a command, not to eat of the tree of the knowledge of good and evil; which while they kept, they were happy in their communion with God, and had dominion over the creatures.

CHAPTER V
Of Providence

I. God the great Creator of all things doth uphold, direct, dispose, and govern all creatures, actions, and things, from the greatest even to the least, by his most wise and holy providence, according to his infallible foreknowledge, and the free and immutable counsel of his own will, to the praise of the glory of his wisdom, power, justice, goodness, and mercy.

II. Although, in relation to the foreknowledge and decree of God, the first Cause, all things come to pass immutably, and infallibly; yet, by the same providence, he ordereth them to fall out, according to the nature of second causes, either necessarily, freely, or contingently.

III. God, in his ordinary providence, maketh use of means, yet is free to work without, above, and against them, at his pleasure.

IV. The almighty power, unsearchable wisdom, and infinite goodness of God so far manifest themselves in his providence, that it extendeth itself even to the first fall, and all other sins of angels and men; and that not by a bare permission, but such as hath joined with it a most wise and powerful bounding, and otherwise ordering, and governing of them, in a manifold dispensation, to his own holy ends; yet so, as the sinfulness thereof proceedeth only from the creature, and not from God, who, being most holy and righteous, neither is nor can be the author or approver of sin.

V. The most wise, righteous, and gracious God doth oftentimes leave, for a season, his own children to manifold temptations, and the corruption of their own hearts, to chastise them for their former sins, or to discover unto them the hidden strength of corruption and deceitfulness of their hearts, that they may be humbled; and, to raise them to a more close and constant dependence for their support upon himself, and to make them more watchful against all future occasions of sin, and for sundry other just and holy ends.

VI. As for those wicked and ungodly men whom God, as a righteous Judge, for former sins, doth blind and harden, from them he not only withholdeth his grace whereby they might have been enlightened in their understandings, and wrought upon in their hearts; but sometimes also withdraweth the gifts which they had, and exposeth them to such objects as their corruption makes occasions of sin; and, withal, gives them over to their own lusts, the temptations of the world, and the power of Satan, whereby it comes to pass that they harden themselves, even under those means which God useth for the softening of others.

VII. As the providence of God doth, in general, reach to all creatures; so, after a most special manner, it taketh care of his church, and disposeth all things to the good thereof.

CHAPTER VI
Of the Fall of Man, of Sin and of the Punishment Thereof

I. Our first parents, being seduced by the subtlety and temptation of Satan, sinned, in eating the forbidden fruit. This their sin, God was pleased, according to his wise and holy counsel, to permit, having purposed to order it to his own glory.

II. By this sin they fell from their original righteousness and communion with God, and so became dead in sin, and wholly defiled in all the parts and faculties of soul and body.

III. They being the root of all mankind, the guilt of this sin was imputed; and the same death in sin, and corrupted nature, conveyed to all their posterity descending from them by ordinary generation.

IV. From this original corruption, whereby we are utterly indisposed, disabled, and made opposite to all good, and wholly inclined to all evil, do proceed all actual transgressions.

V. This corruption of nature, during this life, doth remain in those that are regenerated; and although it be, through Christ, pardoned, and mortified; yet both itself, and all the motions thereof, are truly and properly sin.

VI. Every sin, both original and actual, being a transgression of the righteous law of God, and contrary thereunto, doth, in its own nature, bring guilt upon the sinner, whereby he is bound over to the wrath of God, and curse of the law, and so made subject to death, with all miseries spiritual, temporal, and eternal.

CHAPTER VII
Of God's Covenant with Man

I. The distance between God and the creature is so great, that although reasonable creatures do owe obedience unto him as their Creator, yet they could never have any fruition of him as their blessedness and reward, but by some voluntary condescension on God's part, which he hath been pleased to express by way of covenant.

II. The first covenant made with man was a *covenant of works,* wherein life was promised to Adam; and in him to his posterity, upon condition of perfect and personal obedience.

III. Man, by his fall, having made himself uncapable of life by that covenant, the Lord was pleased to make a second, commonly called the *covenant of grace;* wherein he freely offereth unto sinners life and salvation by Jesus Christ; requiring of them faith in him, that they may be saved, and promising to give unto all those that are ordained unto eternal life his Holy Spirit, to make them willing, and able to believe.

IV. This covenant of grace is frequently set forth in Scripture by the name of a testament, in reference to the death of Jesus Christ the Testator, and to the everlasting inheritance, with all things belonging to it, therein bequeathed.

V. This covenant was differently administered in the time of the law, and in the time of the gospel: under the law, it was administered by promises, prophecies, sacrifices, circumcision, the paschal lamb, and other types and ordinances delivered to the people of the Jews, all foresignifying Christ to come; which were, for that time, sufficient and efficacious, through the operation of the Spirit, to instruct and build up the elect in faith in the promised Messiah, by whom they had full remission of sins, and eternal salvation; and is called the old testament.

VI. Under the gospel, when Christ, the substance, was exhibited, the ordinances in which this covenant is dispensed are the preaching of the Word, and the administration of the sacraments of Baptism and the Lord's Supper: which, though fewer in number, and administered with more simplicity, and less outward glory, yet, in them, it is held forth in more fulness, evidence and spiritual efficacy, to all nations, both Jews and Gentiles; and is called the new testament. There are not therefore two covenants of grace, differing in substance, but one and the same, under various dispensations.

CHAPTER VIII
Of Christ the Mediator

I. It pleased God, in his eternal purpose, to choose and ordain the Lord Jesus, his only begotten Son, to be the Mediator between God and man, the Prophet, Priest, and King, the Head and Savior of his church, the Heir of all things, and Judge of the world: unto whom he did from all eternity give a people, to be his seed, and to be by him in time redeemed, called, justified, sanctified, and glorified.

II. The Son of God, the second person in the Trinity, being very and eternal God, of one substance and equal with the Father, did, when the fulness of time was come, take upon him man's nature, with all the essential properties, and common infirmities thereof, yet without sin; being conceived by the power of the Holy Ghost, in the womb of the virgin Mary, of her substance. So that two whole, perfect, and distinct natures, the Godhead and the manhood, were inseparably joined together in one person, without conversion, composition, or confusion. Which person is very God, and very man, yet one Christ, the only Mediator between God and man.

III. The Lord Jesus, in his human nature thus united to the divine, was sanctified, and anointed with the Holy Spirit, above measure, having in him all the treasures of wisdom and knowledge; in whom it pleased the Father that all fulness should dwell; to the end that, being holy, harmless, undefiled, and full of grace and truth, he might be thoroughly furnished to execute the office of a mediator, and surety. Which office he took not unto himself, but was thereunto called by his Father, who put all power and judgment into his hand, and gave him commandment to execute the same.

IV. This office the Lord Jesus did most willingly undertake; which that he might discharge, he was made under the law, and did perfectly fulfil it; endured most grievous torments immediately in his soul, and most painful sufferings in his body; was crucified, and died, was buried, and remained under the power of death, yet saw no corruption. On the third day he arose from the dead, with the same body in which he suffered, with which also he ascended into heaven, and there sitteth at the right hand of his Father, making intercession, and shall return, to judge men and angels, at the end of the world.

V. The Lord Jesus, by his perfect obedience, and sacrifice of himself, which he, through the eternal Spirit, once offered up unto God, hath fully satisfied the justice of his Father; and purchased, not only reconciliation, but an everlasting inheritance in the kingdom of heaven, for all those whom the Father hath given unto him.

VI. Although the work of redemption was not actually wrought by Christ till after his incarnation, yet the virtue, efficacy, and benefits thereof were communicated unto the elect, in all ages successively from the beginning of the world, in and by those promises, types, and sacrifices, wherein he was revealed, and signified to be the seed of the woman which should bruise the serpent's head; and the Lamb slain from the beginning of the world; being yesterday and today the same, and forever.

VII. Christ, in the work of mediation, acts according to both natures, by each nature doing that which is proper to itself; yet, by reason of the unity of the person, that which is proper to one nature is sometimes in Scripture attributed to the person denominated by the other nature.

VIII. To all those for whom Christ hath purchased redemption, he doth certainly and effectually apply and communicate the same; making intercession for them, and revealing unto them, in and by the Word, the mysteries of salvation; effectually persuading them by his Spirit to believe and obey, and governing their hearts by his Word and Spirit; overcoming all their enemies by his almighty power and wisdom, in such manner, and ways, as are most consonant to his wonderful and unsearchable dispensation.

CHAPTER IX
Of Free Will

I. God hath endued the will of man with that natural liberty, that it is neither forced, nor, by any absolute necessity of nature, determined to good, or evil.

II. Man, in his state of innocency, had freedom, and power to will and to do that which was good and well pleasing to God; but yet, mutably, so that he might fall from it.

III. Man, by his fall into a state of sin, hath wholly lost all ability of will to any spiritual good accompanying salvation: so as, a natural man, being altogether averse from that good, and dead in sin, is not able, by his own strength, to convert himself, or to prepare himself thereunto.

IV. When God converts a sinner, and translates him into the state of grace, he freeth him from his natural bondage under sin; and, by his grace alone, enables him freely to will and to do that which is spiritually good; yet so, as that by reason of his remaining corruption, he doth not perfectly, nor only, will that which is good, but doth also will that which is evil.

V. The will of man is made perfectly and immutably free to good alone, in the state of glory only.

CHAPTER X
Of Effectual Calling

I. All those whom God hath predestinated unto life, and those only, he is pleased, in his appointed and accepted time, effectually to call, by his Word and Spirit, out of that state of sin and death, in which they are by nature, to grace and salvation, by Jesus Christ; enlightening their minds spiritually and savingly to understand the things of God, taking away their heart of stone, and giving unto them a heart of flesh; renewing their wills, and, by his almighty power, determining them to that which is good, and effectually drawing them to Jesus Christ: yet so, as they come most freely, being made willing by his grace.

II. This effectual call is of God's free and special grace alone, not from anything at all foreseen in man, who is altogether passive therein, until, being quickened and renewed by the Holy Spirit, he is thereby enabled to answer this call, and to embrace the grace offered and conveyed in it.

III. Elect infants, dying in infancy, are regenerated, and saved by Christ, through the Spirit, who worketh when, and where, and how he pleaseth: so also are all other elect persons who are uncapable of being outwardly called by the ministry of the Word.

IV. Others, not elected, although they may be called by the ministry of the Word, and may have some common operations of the Spirit, yet they never truly come unto Christ, and therefore cannot be saved: much less can men, not professing the Christian religion, be saved in any other way whatsoever, be they never so diligent to frame their lives according to the light of nature, and the laws of that religion they do profess. And, to assert and maintain that they may, is very pernicious, and to be detested.

CHAPTER XI
Of Justification

I. Those whom God effectually calleth, he also freely justifieth: not by infusing righteousness into them, but by pardoning their sins, and by accounting and accepting their persons as righteous; not for anything wrought in them, or done by them, but for Christ's sake alone; nor by imputing faith itself, the act of believing, or any other evangelical obedience to them, as their righteousness; but by imputing the obedience and satisfaction of Christ unto them, they receiving and resting on him and his righteousness, by faith; which faith they have not of themselves, it is the gift of God.

II. Faith, thus receiving and resting on Christ and his righteousness, is the alone instrument of justification: yet is it not alone in the person justified, but is ever accompanied with all other saving graces, and is no dead faith, but worketh by love.

III. Christ, by his obedience and death, did fully discharge the debt of all those that are thus justified, and did make a proper, real, and full satisfaction to his Father's justice in their behalf. Yet, inasmuch as he was given by the Father for them; and his obedience and satisfaction accepted in their stead; and both, freely, not for anything in them; their justification is only of free grace; that both the exact justice and rich grace of God might be glorified in the justification of sinners.

IV. God did, from all eternity, decree to justify all the elect, and

Christ did, in the fulness of time, die for their sins, and rise again for their justification: nevertheless, they are not justified, until the Holy Spirit doth, in due time, actually apply Christ unto them.

V. God doth continue to forgive the sins of those that are justified; and, although they can never fall from the state of justification, yet they may, by their sins, fall under God's fatherly displeasure, and not have the light of his countenance restored unto them, until they humble themselves, confess their sins, beg pardon, and renew their faith and repentance.

VI. The justification of believers under the old testament was, in all these respects, one and the same with the justification of believers under the new testament.

CHAPTER XII
Of Adoption

I. All those that are justified, God vouchsafeth, in and for his only Son Jesus Christ, to make partakers of the grace of adoption, by which they are taken into the number, and enjoy the liberties and privileges of the children of God, have his name put upon them, receive the spirit of adoption, have access to the throne of grace with boldness, are enabled to cry, Abba, Father, are pitied, protected, provided for, and chastened by him, as by a Father: yet never cast off, but sealed to the day of redemption; and inherit the promises, as heirs of everlasting salvation.

CHAPTER XIII
Of Sanctification

I. They, who are once effectually called, and regenerated, having a new heart, and a new spirit created in them, are further sanctified, really and personally, through the virtue of Christ's death and resurrection, by his Word and Spirit dwelling in them: the dominion of the whole body of sin is destroyed, and the several lusts thereof are more and more weakened and mortified; and they more and more quickened and strengthened in all saving graces, to the practice of true holiness, without which no man shall see the Lord.

II. This sanctification is throughout, in the whole man; yet imperfect in this life, there abiding still some remnants of corruption in every part; whence ariseth a continual and irreconcilable war, the flesh lusting against the Spirit, and the Spirit against the flesh.

III. In which war, although the remaining corruption, for a time, may much prevail; yet, through the continual supply of strength from the sanctifying Spirit of Christ, the regenerate part doth overcome; and so, the saints grow in grace, perfecting holiness in the fear of God.

CHAPTER XIV
Of Saving Faith

I. The grace of faith, whereby the elect are enabled to believe to the saving of their souls, is the work of the Spirit of Christ in their hearts, and is ordinarily wrought by the ministry of the Word, by which also, and by the administration of the sacraments, and prayer, it is increased and strengthened.

II. By this faith, a Christian believeth to be true whatsoever is revealed in the Word, for the authority of God himself speaking therein; and acteth differently upon that which each particular passage thereof containeth; yielding obedience to the commands, trembling at the threatenings, and embracing the promises of God for this life, and that which is to come. But the principal acts of saving faith are accepting, receiving, and resting upon Christ alone for justification, sanctification, and eternal life, by virtue of the covenant of grace.

III. This faith is different in degrees, weak or strong; may be often and many ways assailed, and weakened, but gets the victory: growing up in many to the attainment of a full assurance, through Christ, who is both the author and finisher of our faith.

CHAPTER XV
Of Repentance unto Life

I. Repentance unto life is an evangelical grace, the doctrine whereof is to be preached by every minister of the gospel, as well as that of faith in Christ.

II. By it, a sinner, out of the sight and sense not only of the danger, but also of the filthiness and odiousness of his sins, as contrary to the holy nature, and righteous law of God; and upon the apprehension of his mercy in Christ to such as are penitent, so grieves for, and hates his sins, as to turn from them all unto God, purposing and endeavoring to walk with him in all the ways of his commandments.

III. Although repentance be not to be rested in, as any satisfaction for sin, or any cause of the pardon thereof, which is the act of God's free grace in Christ; yet it is of such necessity to all sinners, that none may expect pardon without it.

IV. As there is no sin so small, but it deserves damnation; so there is no sin so great, that it can bring damnation upon those who truly repent.

V. Men ought not to content themselves with a general repentance, but it is every man's duty to endeavor to repent of his particular sins, particularly.

VI. As every man is bound to make private confession of his sins to God, praying for the pardon thereof; upon which, and the forsaking of them, he shall find mercy; so, he that scandalizeth his brother, or the church of Christ, ought to be willing, by a private or public confession, and sorrow for his sin, to declare his repentance to those that are offended, who are thereupon to be reconciled to him, and in love to receive him.

CHAPTER XVI
Of Good Works

I. Good works are only such as God hath commanded in his holy Word, and not such as, without the warrant thereof, are devised by men, out of blind zeal, or upon any pretense of good intention.

II. These good works, done in obedience to God's commandments, are the fruits and evidences of a true and lively faith: and by them believers manifest their thankfulness, strengthen their assurance, edify their brethren, adorn the profession of the gospel, stop the mouths of the adversaries, and glorify God, whose workmanship they are, created in Christ Jesus thereunto, that, having their fruit unto holiness, they may have the end, eternal life.

III. Their ability to do good works is not at all of themselves, but wholly from the Spirit of Christ. And that they may be enabled thereunto, beside the graces they have already received, there is required an actual influence of the same Holy Spirit, to work in them to will, and to do, of his good pleasure: yet are they not hereupon to grow negligent, as if they were not bound to perform any duty unless upon a special motion of the Spirit; but they ought to be diligent in stirring up the grace of God that is in them.

IV. They who, in their obedience, attain to the greatest height which is possible in this life, are so far from being able to supererogate, and to do more than God requires, as that they fall short of much which in duty they are bound to do.

V. We cannot by our best works merit pardon of sin, or eternal life at the hand of God, by reason of the great disproportion that is between them and the glory to come; and the infinite distance that is between us and God, whom, by them, we can neither profit, nor satisfy for the debt of our former sins, but when we have done all we can, we have done but our duty, and are unprofitable servants: and because, as they are good, they proceed from his Spirit; and as they are wrought by us, they are defiled, and mixed with so much weakness and imperfection, that they cannot endure the severity of God's judgment.

VI. Notwithstanding, the persons of believers being accepted through Christ, their good works also are accepted in him; not as though they were in this life wholly unblamable and unreprovable in God's sight; but that he, looking upon them in his Son, is pleased to accept and reward that which is sincere, although accompanied with many weaknesses and imperfections.

VII. Works done by unregenerate men, although for the matter of them they may be things which God commands; and of good use both to themselves and others: yet, because they proceed not from an heart purified by faith; nor are done in a right manner, according to the Word; nor to a right end, the glory of God, they are therefore sinful, and cannot please God, or make a man meet to receive grace from God: and yet, their neglect of them is more sinful and displeasing unto God.

CHAPTER XVII
Of the Perseverance of the Saints

I. They, whom God hath accepted in his Beloved, effectually called, and sanctified by his Spirit, can neither totally nor finally fall away from the state of grace, but shall certainly persevere therein to the end, and be eternally saved.

II. This perseverance of the saints depends not upon their own free will, but upon the immutability of the decree of election, flowing from the free and unchangeable love of God the Father; upon the efficacy of the merit and intercession of Jesus Christ, the abiding of the Spirit, and of the seed of God within them, and the nature of the covenant of grace: from all which ariseth also the certainty and infallibility thereof.

III. Nevertheless, they may, through the temptations of Satan and of the world, the prevalency of corruption remaining in them, and the neglect of the means of their preservation, fall into grievous sins; and, for a time, continue therein: whereby they incur God's displeasure, and grieve his Holy Spirit, come to be deprived of some measure of their graces and comforts, have their hearts hardened, and their consciences wounded; hurt and scandalize others, and bring temporal judgments upon themselves.

CHAPTER XVIII

Of the Assurance of Grace and Salvation

I. Although hypocrites and other unregenerate men may vainly deceive themselves with false hopes and carnal presumptions of being in the favor of God, and estate of salvation (which hope of theirs shall perish): yet such as truly believe in the Lord Jesus, and love him in sincerity, endeavoring to walk in all good conscience before him, may, in this life, be certainly assured that they are in the state of grace, and may rejoice in the hope of the glory of God, which hope shall never make them ashamed.

II. This certainty is not a bare conjectural and probable persuasion grounded upon a fallible hope; but an infallible assurance of faith founded upon the divine truth of the promises of salvation, the inward evidence of those graces unto which these promises are made, the testimony of the Spirit of adoption witnessing with our spirits that we are the children of God, which Spirit is the earnest of our inheritance, whereby we are sealed to the day of redemption.

III. This infallible assurance doth not so belong to the essence of faith, but that a true believer may wait long, and conflict with many difficulties before he be partaker of it: yet, being enabled by the Spirit to know the things which are freely given him of God, he may, without extraordinary revelation, in the right use of ordinary means, attain thereunto. And therefore it is the duty of everyone to give all diligence to make his calling and election sure, that thereby his heart may be enlarged in peace and joy in the Holy Ghost, in love and thankfulness to God, and in strength and cheerfulness in the duties of obedience, the proper fruits of this assurance; so far is it from inclining men to looseness.

IV. True believers may have the assurance of their salvation divers ways shaken, diminished, and intermitted; as, by negligence in preserving of it, by falling into some special sin which woundeth the conscience and grieveth the Spirit; by some sudden or vehement temptation, by God's withdrawing the light of his countenance, and suffering even such as fear him to walk in darkness and to have no light: yet are they never utterly destitute of that seed of God, and life of faith, that love of Christ and the brethren, that sincerity of heart, and conscience of duty, out of which, by the operation of the Spirit, this assurance may, in due time, be revived; and by the which, in the meantime, they are supported from utter despair.

CHAPTER XIX
Of the Law of God

I. God gave to Adam a law, as a covenant of works, by which he bound him and all his posterity to personal, entire, exact, and perpetual obedience, promised life upon the fulfilling, and threatened death upon the breach of it, and endued him with power and ability to keep it.

II. This law, after his fall, continued to be a perfect rule of righteousness; and, as such, was delivered by God upon Mount Sinai, in ten commandments, and written in two tables: the four first commandments containing our duty towards God; and the other six, our duty to man.

III. Beside this law, commonly called *moral,* God was pleased to give to the people of Israel, as a church under age, ceremonial laws, containing several typical ordinances, partly of worship, prefiguring Christ, his graces, actions, sufferings, and benefits; and partly, holding forth divers instructions of moral duties. All which ceremonial laws are now abrogated, under the new testament.

IV. To them also, as a body politic, he gave sundry judicial laws, which expired together with the state of that people; not obliging any other now, further than the general equity thereof may require.

V. The moral law doth forever bind all, as well justified persons as others, to the obedience thereof; and that, not only in regard of the matter contained in it, but also in respect of the authority of God the Creator, who gave it. Neither doth Christ, in the Gospel, any way dissolve, but much strengthen this obligation.

VI. Although true believers be not under the law, as a covenant of works, to be thereby justified, or condemned; yet is it of great use to them, as well as to others; in that, as a rule of life informing them of the will of God, and their duty, it directs and binds them to walk accordingly; discovering also the sinful pollutions of their nature, hearts, and lives; so as, examining themselves thereby, they may come to further conviction of, humiliation for, and hatred against sin, together with a clearer sight of the need they have of Christ, and the perfection of his obedience. It is likewise of use to the regenerate, to restrain their corruptions, in that it forbids sin: and the threatenings of it serve to show what even their sins deserve; and what afflictions, in this life, they may expect for them, although freed from the curse thereof threatened in the law. The promises of it, in like manner, show them God's approbation of obedience, and what blessings they may expect upon the performance thereof: although not as due to them by the law as a covenant of works. So as, a man's doing good, and refraining from evil, because the law encourageth to the one, and deterreth from the other, is no evidence of his being under the law; and, not under grace.

VII. Neither are the forementioned uses of the law contrary to the grace of the gospel, but do sweetly comply with it; the Spirit of Christ subduing and enabling the will of man to do that freely, and cheerfully, which the will of God, revealed in the law, requireth to be done.

CHAPTER XX
Of Christian Liberty and Liberty of Conscience

I. The liberty which Christ hath purchased for believers under the gospel consists in their freedom from the guilt of sin, the condemning wrath of God, the curse of the moral law; and, in their being delivered from this present evil world, bondage to Satan, and dominion of sin; from the evil of afflictions, the sting of death, the victory of the grave, and everlasting damnation; as also, in their free access to God, and their yielding obedience unto him, not out of slavish fear, but a childlike love and willing mind. All which were common also to believers under the law. But, under the new testament, the liberty of Christians is further enlarged, in their freedom from the yoke of the ceremonial law, to which the Jewish church was subjected; and in greater boldness of access to the throne of grace, and in fuller communications of the free Spirit of God, than believers under the law did ordinarily partake of.

II. God alone is Lord of the conscience, and hath left it free from the doctrines and commandments of men, which are, in anything, contrary to his Word; or beside it, if matters of faith, or worship. So that, to believe such doctrines, or to obey such commands, out of conscience, is to betray true liberty of conscience: and the requiring of an implicit faith, and an absolute and blind obedience, is to destroy liberty of conscience, and reason also.

III. They who, upon pretense of Christian liberty, do practice any sin, or cherish any lust, do thereby destroy the end of Christian liberty, which is, that being delivered out of the hands of our enemies, we might serve the Lord without fear, in holiness and righteousness before him, all the days of our life.

IV. And because the powers which God hath ordained, and the liberty which Christ hath purchased, are not intended by God to destroy, but mutually to uphold and preserve one another, they who, upon pretense of Christian liberty, shall oppose any lawful power, or the lawful exercise of it, whether it be civil or ecclesiastical, resist the ordinance of God. And, for their publishing of such opinions, or maintaining of such practices, as are contrary to the light of nature, or to the known principles of Christianity (whether concerning faith, worship, or conversation), or to the power of godliness; or, such erroneous opinions or practices, as either in their own nature, or in the manner of publishing or maintaining them, are destructive to the external peace and order which Christ hath established in the church, they may lawfully be called to account, and proceeded against, by the censures of the church.

CHAPTER XXI
Of Religious Worship and the Sabbath Day

I. The light of nature showeth that there is a God, who hath lordship and sovereignty over all, is good, and doth good unto all, and is therefore to be feared, loved, praised, called upon, trusted in, and served, with all the heart, and with all the soul, and with all the might. But the acceptable way of worshiping the true God is instituted by himself, and so limited by his own revealed will, that he may not be worshiped according to the imaginations and devices of men, or the suggestions of Satan, under any visible representation, or any other way not prescribed in the holy Scripture.

II. Religious worship is to be given to God, the Father, Son, and Holy Ghost; and to him alone; not to angels, saints, or any other creature: and, since the fall, not without a Mediator; nor in the mediation of any other but of Christ alone.

III. Prayer, with thanksgiving, being one special part of religious worship, is by God required of all men: and, that it may be accepted, it is to be made in the name of the Son, by the help of his Spirit, according to his will, with understanding, reverence, humility, fervency, faith, love, and perseverance; and, if vocal, in a known tongue.

IV. Prayer is to be made for things lawful; and for all sorts of men living, or that shall live hereafter: but not for the dead, nor for those of whom it may be known that they have sinned the sin unto death.

V. The reading of the Scriptures with godly fear, the sound preaching and conscionable hearing of the Word, in obedience unto God, with understanding, faith, and reverence, singing of psalms with grace in the heart; as also, the due administration and worthy receiving of the sacraments instituted by Christ, are all parts of the ordinary religious worship of God: beside religious oaths, vows, solemn fastings, and thanksgivings upon special occasions, which are, in their several times and seasons, to be used in an holy and religious manner.

VI. Neither prayer, nor any other part of religious worship, is now, under the gospel, either tied unto, or made more acceptable by any place in which it is performed, or towards which it is directed: but God is to be worshiped everywhere, in spirit and truth; as, in private families daily, and in secret, each one by himself; so, more solemnly in the public assemblies, which are not carelessly or wilfully to be neglected, or forsaken, when God, by his Word or providence, calleth thereunto.

VII. As it is the law of nature, that, in general, a due proportion of time be set apart for the worship of God; so, in his Word, by a positive, moral, and perpetual commandment binding all men in all ages, he hath particularly appointed one day in seven, for a sabbath, to be kept holy unto him: which, from the beginning of the world to the resurrection of Christ, was the last day of the week; and, from the resurrection of Christ, was changed into the first day of the week, which, in Scripture, is called the Lord's day, and is to be continued to the end of the world, as the Christian sabbath.

VIII. This sabbath is then kept holy unto the Lord, when men, after a due preparing of their hearts, and ordering of their common affairs beforehand, do not only observe an holy rest, all the day, from their own works, words, and thoughts about their worldly employments and recreations, but also are taken up, the whole time, in the public and private exercises of his worship, and in the duties of necessity and mercy.

CHAPTER XXII
Of Lawful Oaths and Vows

I. A lawful oath is a part of religious worship, wherein, upon just occasion, the person swearing solemnly calleth God to witness what he asserteth, or promiseth, and to judge him according to the truth or falsehood of what he sweareth.

II. The name of God only is that by which men ought to swear, and therein it is to be used with all holy fear and reverence. Therefore, to swear vainly, or rashly, by that glorious and dreadful Name; or, to swear at all by any other thing, is sinful, and to be abhorred. Yet, as in matters of weight and moment, an oath is warranted by the Word of God, under the new testament as well as under the old; so a lawful oath, being imposed by lawful authority, in such matters, ought to be taken.

III. Whosoever taketh an oath ought duly to consider the weightiness of so solemn an act, and therein to avouch nothing but what he is fully persuaded is the truth: neither may any man bind himself by oath to anything but what is good and just, and what he believeth so to be, and what he is able and resolved to perform.

IV. An oath is to be taken in the plain and common sense of the words, without equivocation, or mental reservation. It cannot oblige to sin; but in anything not sinful, being taken, it binds to performance, although to a man's own hurt. Nor is it to be violated, although made to heretics, or infidels.

V. A vow is of the like nature with a promissory oath, and ought to be made with the like religious care, and to be performed with the like faithfulness.

VI. It is not to be made to any creature, but to God alone: and, that it may be accepted, it is to be made voluntarily, out of faith, and conscience of duty, in way of thankfulness for mercy received, or for the obtaining of what we want, whereby we more strictly bind ourselves to necessary duties; or, to other things, so far and so long as they may fitly conduce thereunto.

VII. No man may vow to do anything forbidden in the Word of God, or what would hinder any duty therein commanded, or which is not in his own power, and for the performance whereof he hath no promise of ability from God. In which respects, popish monastical vows of perpetual single life, professed poverty, and regular obedience, are so far from being degrees of higher perfection, that they are superstitious and sinful snares, in which no Christian may entangle himself.

CHAPTER XXIII
Of the Civil Magistrate

I. God, the supreme Lord and King of all the world, hath ordained civil magistrates, to be, under him, over the people, for his own glory, and the public good: and, to this end, hath armed them with the power of the sword, for the defense and encouragement of them that are good, and for the punishment of evil doers.

II. It is lawful for Christians to accept and execute the office of a magistrate, when called thereunto: in the managing whereof, as they ought especially to maintain piety, justice, and peace, according to the wholesome laws of each commonwealth; so, for that end, they may lawfully, now under the new testament, wage war, upon just and necessary occasion.

III. Civil magistrates may not assume to themselves the administration of the Word and sacraments; or the power of the keys of the kingdom of heaven; or, in the least, interfere in matters of faith. Yet, as nursing fathers, it is the duty of civil magistrates to protect the church of our common Lord, without giving the preference to any denomination of Christians above the rest, in such a manner that all ecclesiastical persons whatever shall enjoy the full, free, and unquestioned liberty of discharging every part of their sacred functions, without violence or danger. And, as Jesus Christ hath appointed a regular government and discipline in his church, no law of any commonwealth should interfere with, let, or hinder, the due exercise thereof, among the voluntary members of *any* denomination of Christians, according to their own profession and belief. It is the duty of civil magistrates to protect the person and good name of all their people, in such an effectual manner as that no person be suffered, either upon pretense of religion or of infidelity, to offer any indignity, violence, abuse, or injury to any other person whatsoever: and to take order, that all religious and ecclesiastical assemblies be held without molestation or disturbance.

IV. It is the duty of people to pray for magistrates, to honor their persons, to pay them tribute or other dues, to obey their lawful commands, and to be subject to their authority, for conscience' sake. Infidelity, or difference in religion, doth not make void the magistrates' just and legal authority, nor free the people from their due obedience to them: from which ecclesiastical persons are not exempted, much less hath the pope any power and jurisdiction over them in their dominions, or over any of their people; and, least of all, to deprive them of their dominions, or lives, if he shall judge them to be heretics, or upon any other pretense whatsoever.

CHAPTER XXIV
Of Marriage and Divorce

I. Marriage is to be between one man and one woman: neither is it lawful for any man to have more than one wife, nor for any woman to have more than one husband, at the same time.

II. Marriage was ordained for the mutual help of husband and wife, for the increase of mankind with legitimate issue, and of the church with an holy seed; and for preventing of uncleanness.

III. It is lawful for all sorts of people to marry, who are able with judgment to give their consent. Yet it is the duty of Christians to marry only in the Lord. And therefore such as profess the true reformed religion should not marry with infidels, papists, or other idolaters: neither should such as are godly be unequally yoked, by marrying with such as are notoriously wicked in their life, or maintain damnable heresies.

IV. Marriage ought not to be within the degrees of consanguinity or affinity forbidden by the Word. Nor can such incestuous marriages ever be made lawful by any law of man or consent of parties, so as those persons may live together as man and wife.

V. Adultery or fornication committed after a contract, being detected before marriage, giveth just occasion to the innocent party to dissolve that contract. In the case of adultery after marriage, it is lawful for the innocent party to sue out a divorce: and, after the divorce, to marry another, as if the offending party were dead.

VI. Although the corruption of man be such as is apt to study arguments unduly to put asunder those whom God hath joined together in marriage: yet, nothing but adultery, or such wilful desertion as can no way be remedied by the church, or civil magistrate, is cause sufficient of dissolving the bond of marriage: wherein, a public and orderly course of proceeding is to be observed; and the persons concerned in it not left to their own wills, and discretion, in their own case.

CHAPTER XXV
Of the Church

I. The catholic or universal church, which is invisible, consists of the whole number of the elect, that have been, are, or shall be gathered into one, under Christ the head thereof; and is the spouse, the body, the fulness of him that filleth all in all.

II. The visible church, which is also catholic or universal under the gospel (not confined to one nation, as before under the law), consists of all those throughout the world that profess the true religion; and of their children: and is the kingdom of the Lord Jesus Christ, the house and family of God, out of which there is no ordinary possibility of salvation.

III. Unto this catholic visible church Christ hath given the ministry, oracles, and ordinances of God, for the gathering and perfecting of the saints, in this life, to the end of the world: and doth, by his own presence and Spirit, according to his promise, make them effectual thereunto.

IV. This catholic church hath been sometimes more, sometimes less visible. And particular churches, which are members thereof, are more or less pure, according as the doctrine of the gospel is taught and embraced, ordinances administered, and public worship performed more or less purely in them.

V. The purest churches under heaven are subject both to mixture and error; and some have so degenerated, as to become no churches of Christ, but synagogues of Satan. Nevertheless, there shall be always a church on earth, to worship God according to his will.

VI. There is no other head of the church but the Lord Jesus Christ. Nor can the pope of Rome, in any sense, be head thereof.

CHAPTER XXVI
Of the Communion of Saints

I. All saints, that are united to Jesus Christ their head, by his Spirit, and by faith, have fellowship with him in his graces, sufferings, death, resurrection, and glory: and, being united to one another in love, they have communion in each other's gifts and graces, and are obliged to the performance of such duties, public and private, as do conduce to their mutual good, both in the inward and outward man.

II. Saints by profession are bound to maintain an holy fellowship and communion in the worship of God, and in performing such other spiritual services as tend to their mutual edification; as also in relieving each other in outward things, according to their several abilities and necessities. Which communion, as God offereth opportunity, is to be extended unto all those who, in every place, call upon the name of the Lord Jesus.

III. This communion which the saints have with Christ, doth not make them in any wise partakers of the substance of his Godhead; or to be equal with Christ in any respect: either of which to affirm is impious and blasphemous. Nor doth their communion one with another, as saints, take away, or infringe the title or propriety which each man hath in his goods and possessions.

CHAPTER XXVII
Of the Sacraments

I. Sacraments are holy signs and seals of the covenant of grace, immediately instituted by God, to represent Christ, and his benefits; and to confirm our interest in him: as also, to put a visible difference between those that belong unto the church, and the rest of the world; and solemnly to engage them to the service of God in Christ, according to his Word.

II. There is, in every sacrament, a spiritual relation, or sacramental union, between the sign and the thing signified: whence it comes to pass, that the names and effects of the one are attributed to the other.

III. The grace which is exhibited in or by the sacraments rightly used, is not conferred by any power in them; neither doth the efficacy of a sacrament depend upon the piety or intention of him that doth administer it: but upon the work of the Spirit, and the word of institution, which contains, together with a precept authorizing the use thereof, a promise of benefit to worthy receivers.

IV. There be only two sacraments ordained by Christ our Lord in the gospel; that is to say, Baptism, and the Supper of the Lord: neither of which may be dispensed by any, but by a minister of the Word lawfully ordained.

V. The sacraments of the old testament, in regard of the spiritual things thereby signified and exhibited, were, for substance, the same with those of the new.

CHAPTER XXVIII
Of Baptism

I. Baptism is a sacrament of the new testament, ordained by Jesus Christ, not only for the solemn admission of the party baptized into the visible church; but also, to be unto him a sign and seal of the covenant of grace, of his ingrafting into Christ, of regeneration, of remission of sins, and of his giving up unto God, through Jesus Christ, to walk in newness of life. Which sacrament is, by Christ's own appointment, to be continued in his church until the end of the world.

II. The outward element to be used in this sacrament is water, wherewith the party is to be baptized, in the name of the Father, and of the Son, and of the Holy Ghost, by a minister of the gospel, lawfully called thereunto.

III. Dipping of the person into the water is not necessary; but Baptism is rightly administered by pouring, or sprinkling water upon the person.

IV. Not only those that do actually profess faith in and obedience unto Christ, but also the infants of one, or both, believing parents, are to be baptized.

V. Although it be a great sin to contemn or neglect this ordinance, yet grace and salvation are not so inseparably annexed unto it, as that no person can be regenerated, or saved, without it; or, that all that are baptized are undoubtedly regenerated.

VI. The efficacy of Baptism is not tied to that moment of time wherein it is administered; yet, notwithstanding, by the right use of this ordinance, the grace promised is not only offered, but really exhibited, and conferred, by the Holy Ghost, to such (whether of age or infants) as that grace belongeth unto, according to the counsel of God's own will, in his appointed time.

VII. The sacrament of Baptism is but once to be administered unto any person.

CHAPTER XXIX
Of the Lord's Supper

I. Our Lord Jesus, in the night wherein he was betrayed, instituted the sacrament of his body and blood, called the Lord's Supper, to be observed in his church, unto the end of the world, for the perpetual remembrance of the sacrifice of himself in his death; the sealing all benefits thereof unto true believers, their spiritual nourishment and growth in him, their further engagement in and to all duties which they owe unto him; and, to be a bond and pledge of their communion with him, and with each other, as members of his mystical body.

II. In this sacrament, Christ is not offered up to his Father; nor any real sacrifice made at all, for remission of sins of the quick or dead; but only a commemoration of that one offering up of himself, by himself, upon the cross, once for all: and a spiritual oblation of all possible praise unto God, for the same: so that the popish sacrifice of the mass (as they call it) is most abominably injurious to Christ's one, only sacrifice, the alone propitiation for all the sins of his elect.

III. The Lord Jesus hath, in this ordinance, appointed his ministers to declare his word of institution to the people; to pray, and bless the elements of bread and wine, and thereby to set them apart from a common to an holy use; and to take and break the bread, to take the cup, and (they communicating also themselves) to give both to the communicants; but to none who are not then present in the congregation.

IV. Private masses, or receiving this sacrament by a priest, or any other, alone; as likewise, the denial of the cup to the people, worshiping the elements, the lifting them up, or carrying them about, for adoration, and the reserving them for any pretended religious use; are all contrary to the nature of this sacrament, and to the institution of Christ.

V. The outward elements in this sacrament, duly set apart to the uses ordained by Christ, have such relation to him crucified, as that, truly, yet sacramentally only, they are sometimes called by the name of the things they present, to wit, the body and blood of Christ; albeit, in substance and nature, they still remain truly and only bread and wine, as they were before.

VI. That doctrine which maintains a change of the substance of bread and wine into the substance of Christ's body and blood (commonly called *transubstantiation*) by consecration of a priest, or by any other way, is repugnant, not to Scripture alone, but even to common sense, and reason; overthroweth the nature of the sacrament, and hath been, and is, the cause of manifold superstitions; yea, of gross idolatries.

VII. Worthy receivers, outwardly partaking of the visible elements, in this sacrament, do then also, inwardly by faith, really and indeed, yet not carnally and corporally but spiritually, receive, and feed upon, Christ crucified, and all benefits of his death: the body and blood of Christ being then, not corporally or carnally, in, with, or under the bread and wine; yet, as really, but spiritually, present to the faith of believers in that ordinance, as the elements themselves are to their outward senses.

VIII. Although ignorant and wicked men receive the outward elements in this sacrament; yet, they receive not the thing signified thereby; but, by their unworthy coming thereunto, are guilty of the body and blood of the Lord, to their own damnation. Wherefore, all ignorant and ungodly persons, as they are unfit to enjoy communion with him, so are they unworthy of the Lord's table; and cannot, without great sin against Christ, while they remain such, partake of these holy mysteries, or be admitted thereunto.

CHAPTER XXX
Of Church Censures

I. The Lord Jesus, as king and head of his church, hath therein appointed a government, in the hand of church officers, distinct from the civil magistrate.

II. To these officers the keys of the kingdom of heaven are committed; by virtue whereof, they have power, respectively, to retain, and remit sins; to shut that kingdom against the impenitent, both by the Word, and censures; and to open it unto penitent sinners, by the ministry of the gospel; and by absolution from censures, as occasion shall require.

III. Church censures are necessary, for the reclaiming and gaining of offending brethren, for deterring of others from the like offenses, for purging out of that leaven which might infect the whole lump, for vindicating the honor of Christ, and the holy profession of the gospel, and for preventing the wrath of God, which might justly fall upon the church, if they should suffer his covenant, and the seals thereof, to be profaned by notorious and obstinate offenders.

IV. For the better attaining of these ends, the officers of the church are to proceed by admonition; suspension from the sacrament of the Lord's Supper for a season; and by excommunication from the church; according to the nature of the crime, and demerit of the person.

CHAPTER XXXI
Of Synods and Councils

I. For the better government, and further edification of the church, there ought to be such assemblies as are commonly called *synods* or *councils:* and it belongeth to the overseers and other rulers of the particular churches, by virtue of their office, and the power which Christ hath given them for edification and not for destruction, to appoint such assemblies; and to convene together in them, as often as they shall judge it expedient for the good of the church.

II. It belongeth to synods and councils, ministerially to determine controversies of faith, and cases of conscience; to set down rules and directions for the better ordering of the public worship of God, and government of his church; to receive complaints in cases of maladministration, and authoritatively to determine the same: which decrees and determinations, if consonant to the Word of God, are to be received with reverence and submission; not only for their agreement with the Word, but also for the power whereby they are made, as being an ordinance of God appointed thereunto in his Word.

III. All synods or councils, since the apostles' times, whether general or particular, may err; and many have erred. Therefore they are not to be made the rule of faith, or practice; but to be used as a help in both.

IV. Synods and councils are to handle, or conclude nothing, but that which is ecclesiastical: and are not to intermeddle with civil affairs which concern the commonwealth, unless by way of humble petition in cases extraordinary; or, by way of advice, for satisfaction of conscience, if they be thereunto required by the civil magistrate.

CHAPTER XXXII
Of the State of Men after Death, and of the
Resurrection of the Dead

I. The bodies of men, after death, return to dust, and see corruption:

but their souls, which neither die nor sleep, having an immortal sub-
sistence, immediately return to God who gave them: the souls of the
righteous, being then made perfect in holiness, are received into the
highest heavens, where they behold the face of God, in light and
glory, waiting for the full redemption of their bodies. And the souls
of the wicked are cast into hell, where they remain in torments and
utter darkness, reserved to the judgment of the great day. Beside
these two places, for souls separated from their bodies, the Scripture
acknowledgeth none.

II. At the last day, such as are found alive shall not die, but be
changed: and all the dead shall be raised up, with the selfsame bodies,
and none other (although with different qualities), which shall be
united again to their souls forever.

III. The bodies of the unjust shall, by the power of Christ, be raised
to dishonor: the bodies of the just, by his Spirit, unto honor; and be
made conformable to his own glorious body.

CHAPTER XXXIII
Of the Last Judgment

I. God hath appointed a day, wherein he will judge the world, in
righteousness, by Jesus Christ, to whom all power and judgment is
given of the Father. In which day, not only the apostate angels shall
be judged, but likewise all persons that have lived upon earth shall
appear before the tribunal of Christ, to give an account of their
thoughts, words, and deeds; and to receive according to what they
have done in the body, whether good or evil.

II. The end of God's appointing this day is for the manifestation of
the glory of his mercy, in the eternal salvation of the elect; and of his
justice, in the damnation of the reprobate, who are wicked and dis-
obedient. For then shall the righteous go into everlasting life, and
receive that fulness of joy and refreshing, which shall come from the
presence of the Lord; but the wicked who know not God, and obey

not the gospel of Jesus Christ, shall be cast into eternal torments, and be punished with everlasting destruction from the presence of the Lord, and from the glory of his power.

III. As Christ would have us to be certainly persuaded that there shall be a day of judgment, both to deter all men from sin; and for the greater consolation of the godly in their adversity: so will he have that day unknown to men, that they may shake off all carnal security, and be always watchful, because they know not at what hour the Lord will come; and may be ever prepared to say, Come Lord Jesus, come quickly, Amen.

Finis.

REVIEW AND STUDY GUIDE

INTRODUCTION

*T*he purpose of the Foundations of the Faith series is to reacquaint the reader with some of the great doctrines and favorite Scripture passages relating to our Christian life. Indeed, these books attempt to link together our faith as we understand it and our life as we live it. Though our goal is to provide more in-depth teaching on a topic, we hope to accomplish this with a popular style and practical application. Books in the series include the Lord's Prayer, the Ten Commandments, Psalm 23, and 1 Corinthians 13.

In keeping with our goal of a popular-level treatment, this review and study guide is not meant to involve exhaustive digging, but to reinforce the important concepts in the "Points to Consider" and to help you explore some of their implications in the "Question and Response."

A book's impact is judged in the long term, and if you can retain at least one important point per chapter and answer and act upon some of the questions relevant to your life, you have made considerable progress. May God bless your walk with Him as you enter into these exercises.

JAMES S. BELL, JR.

Chapter One

POINTS TO CONSIDER

1. General revelation is what God shows us in creation related to His power, wisdom, and beauty.

2. Science cannot reveal truth or moral absolutes, but can only analyze and quantify the material world.

3. God has given to us a clear and authoritative record of Himself and His will for us in the Holy Scriptures.

4. As we read the Scriptures they become more credible, and as we do what they say we realize their internal consistency.

5. We need to learn how to interpret the Scriptures carefully; but, more importantly, we need to let them transform our lives.

QUESTIONS AND RESPONSE

1. What one thing most proved to you that the Bible was God's Word, without error, and able to reveal the secrets of your heart?

2. Have you sought God for a systematic and effective plan to study and apply His Word?

Chapter Two

1. Much of what we observe makes it appear that God is not in control—whether it's natural disasters, senseless violence, or lack of justice.

2. Just as we can't advise the top golf pro how to play his game, in the same way it makes no sense to tell God how to run the universe.

3. God is like the author of a book, where nothing can occur unless it originates in His own mind.

4. Though God's control is larger than our freedom, nonetheless our choices are still free, being used completely within His purposes.

5. There is great comfort in knowing that the Scriptures tell us over and over that no matter what threatens us, God is able to overcome it.

QUESTIONS AND RESPONSE

1. In what areas do you most question God's running of the universe? Confess your presumption and seek greater understanding from His Word.

2. Is there a situation in your life now that seems to be out of God's control? Confess your trust in His sovereignty and willingness to obey His will.

Chapter Three

1. If people were basically good we would have less of a need for law courts, psychologists, and the like.

2. Because we are made in the image of God we have the potential for great good, but because we are fallen we are capable of great evil as well.

3. We alone in the entire creation can reflect His person and glory, because we are the only creatures that reflect His image.

4. Total depravity does not mean we are as bad as we can be, but rather that every aspect of our nature has been corrupted.

5. Though we fall sadly short of achieving the potential God made us for, He does not abandon us but redeems us instead.

QUESTIONS AND RESPONSE

1. Recount some adverse effects in our society when we operate under the premise that people are basically good.

2. Where in your own life have you run into trouble by assuming that your own motives or actions were totally pure?

Chapter Four

1. Though we live in a complex world where it's hard to determine cause and effect, we have continual liberty of choice that does not undercut God's sovereignty.

2. Actions can be freely chosen and yet the outcomes may be certain, because they are in harmony with the person making the choice.

3. When we fall into sin we are incapable of returning to God, so His sovereign choice to redeem us in our helplessness is great news.

4. God will not allow anything to get in the way of His work of saving from hell the souls He has chosen.

5. The doctrine of predestination can give us a sense of security, peace, patience, and courage, as we step out in God's foolproof plan.

Questions and Response

1. Most of us have at least some difficulty with the doctrine of predestination. What problems has this chapter cleared up for you?

2. How would you now answer the accusation that those condemned to hell have no choice?

Chapter Five

POINTS TO CONSIDER

1. The covenant of grace does not mean that God lets us off the hook but that He transforms us by His power.

2. Jesus Christ clearly reflects the very essence of God, being completely identified with His nature in every way.

3. Each member of the Godhead shares completely in the divine nature but differs according to the expression or Person within the Godhead.

4. Because Jesus has two natures, He can express Himself sometimes through His divine and sometimes through His human nature.

5. Having been tempted in the flesh, Jesus sympathizes with us as sinners, but having a divine nature He is also able to overcome temptation.

QUESTIONS AND RESPONSE

1. Name at least two cases each where Jesus expressed His human and divine natures in Scripture.

2. How would you best describe how you personally abide in Christ, or what brings you closest to Him?

Chapter Six

1. The refusal to admit our sin in and of itself shows us how morally bankrupt we are and hinders our ability to change.

2. God is uncompromising in dealing with sin because it violates His holiness and He is aware of its devastating consequences in our lives.

3. Justification is not a matter of improving our own righteousness to stand before a holy God, but obtaining His righteousness found in Christ.

4. When we are justified, Christ's power and life surge through us like a strong transplanted heart in place of a weak one.

5. Being justified because He paid for our sin—past, present, and future—does not mean that we can sin whenever we wish and suffer no consequences.

QUESTIONS AND RESPONSE

1. How is it that if we continue to sin (which all of us do) we can still be justified in the sight of God?

2. The author tells us what it means to trust in Jesus. Write down the things you trust Jesus for in your life. In what areas do you fall short?

Chapter Seven

1. Adoption into God's family is a neglected but very exciting teaching because we can approach Him as our intimate Father.

2. The doctrine of adoption goes beyond empty self-esteem, telling us we are of infinite worth in the family of God.

3. It is a wonderful privilege to be able to talk to God as our Father at any time and have Him give us His full attention.

4. God does not punish us, because He has dealt with our sin, but He does discipline us for training purposes.

5. We don't need to look to our feelings to know of God's great love for us; rather, as we look to Him the Holy Spirit will work in us to His good pleasure.

QUESTIONS AND RESPONSE

1. Do you normally sense God's affection toward you as similar to your feelings for your own child or parent?

2. How do you handle setbacks or trials if you know you are a part of the family of God?

Chapter Eight

Points to Consider

1. Sanctification takes away sin's mastery of us, then weakens its grip, and finally brings us to complete holiness.

2. There is no instant—or even easy—holiness, because it is a struggle to give up the old desires of the flesh.

3. We subconsciously think that through discipline and skill we can become holy, but it is only the power of God's Spirit that achieves this.

4. There must be a cooperative venture between ourselves and the Holy Spirit; our deliberate acts of obedience are made possible by Him.

5. Our task is a large one: to concentrate our entire resources of mind, heart, and will on full union with Jesus Christ.

Questions and Response

1. What are some of the false views of sanctification promoted throughout church history or in the present day?

2. How can you better learn to cooperate with the Holy Spirit rather than run your own holiness program?

Chapter Nine

1. Repentance is to release to God the sin that cannot hold us because God has released us from its power.

2. Faith is not mere belief, but also is a trust in the object of that belief and a willingness to act upon it.

3. Commitment does not just mean our own self-generated actions, but our willingness to cast ourselves on God and let Him carry us.

4. If we continue to resist God instead of repenting, eventually He will let us see that our self-sufficiency is disastrous.

5. God is capable of doing anything in us by the power of His Spirit if we repent, trust, and obey.

QUESTIONS AND RESPONSE

1. When has your repentance merely involved sorrow but still lacked the sense of the futility of your own sufficiency?

2. Name a time in your life when you thought you could get through a dangerous situation by yourself but God proved that only He could do it.

Chapter Ten

POINTS TO CONSIDER

1. If we believe we are saved and then do as we please, we are deceived, because if we don't bear fruit we demonstrate that we are dead spiritually.

2. Perseverance does not mean that everyone who merely names Christ as Savior based on some emotional experience will last to the end.

3. A true believer is not one who makes an initial confession but one who does the works of God consistently.

4. We should not allow mere stumbling or a host of setbacks to make us believe that we will never persevere to the end.

5. This doctrine is both a serious warning and a wonderful promise—we must and will endure to the end, whatever it takes.

QUESTIONS AND RESPONSE

1. Where along the spectrum do you stand in having confidence that you will bear fruit as a Christian to the end of your life?

2. What are the major challenges, fears, weaknesses, etc., that make you sometimes doubt perseverance?

Chapter Eleven

POINTS TO CONSIDER

1. As we worship on Sunday, we are often unaware of the vital role we play in the outcome of the great cosmic battle between good and evil.

2. What made Israel unique is that God continually dwelt among them, rather than being unapproachable or far off.

3. Now Christ indwells each believer in a way that goes far beyond God's presence in the tabernacle in the wilderness with the Israelites.

4. As Christ indwells each of us, He creates a corporate dwelling place for God's Spirit, a holy temple that is unique in the world.

5. The great community of saints who worship God encompasses not only the globe, but the history of the church, including the Old Testament faithful.

QUESTIONS AND RESPONSE

1. What importance does the church have in your own faith and practice?

2. If the church is so imperfect, how does God effectively manifest His presence through it?

Chapter Twelve

POINTS TO CONSIDER

1. Today the world gets increasingly dark and we become more vulnerable to a multitude of problems threatening to engulf us.

2. Without intervention from God we could only be aware of our present human condition as the norm, without realizing the full potential for good that believers possess.

3. At the end of time we will have both unrestrained evil and a devastating judgment, so we must be made ready.

4. God is going to judge every aspect of our thoughts, words, and behavior; so we need to be extremely circumspect in our living.

5. The good of our present creation will not disappear in the judgment but will be made perfect forever.

QUESTIONS AND RESPONSE

1. Regarding your own life, what are you most looking forward to at the "Last Judgment"? What are you least looking forward to?

2. Would you agree that the evil found in our culture today is of a greater magnitude than evil manifestations from the past?